DAVID WEATHERLY

MONSTERS OF THE HAWKEYE STATE:

CRYPTIDS & LEGENDS
OF
IOWA
FOREWORD BY KEVIN LEE NELSON

Eerie Lights Publishing
Eerielights.com
Eerielightspublishing.com

DAVID WEATHERLY
MONSTERS OF THE HAWKEYE STATE:
CRYPTIDS & LEGENDS
OF
IOWA
FOREWORD BY KEVIN LEE NELSON

Based on interviews and research conducted by David Weatherly

ISBN: 978-1-945950-36-0 (Paperback)

Published by:

EERIE LIGHTS
Eerie Lights Publishing
Eerielightspublishing.com

Cover design: Sam Shearon
www.mister-sam.com

Editor: Jerry Hajewski

Book layout/design: SMAK
www.smakgraphics.com

Printed in the United States of America

Also by David Weatherly

Strange Intruders
Eerie Companions: A History of Haunted Dolls
Black Eyed Children

Silver State Monsters: Cryptids & Legends of Nevada
Copper State Monsters: Cryptids & Legends of Arizona
Monsters of the Last Frontier: Cryptids & Legends of Alaska
Monsters at the Crossroads: Cryptids & Legends of Indiana
Monsters of the Tar Heel State: Cryptids & Legends of North Carolina
Peach State Monsters: Cryptids & Legends of Georgia
Monsters of Big Sky Country: Cryptids & Legends of Montana
Palmetto State Monsters: Cryptids & Legends of South Carolina
Beehive State Monsters: Cryptids & Legends of Utah

The Haunted Series (co-authored with Ross Allison)
Haunted Toys
Haunted Ships & Lighthouses
Haunted Churches
Haunted Prisons
Haunted Historic Hotels of the Pacific Coast

Shadow Chaser (co-authored with Sean Austin)
Shadow Chaser The In-Between (co-authored with Sean Austin)
Paranormal Files: West Virginia

Wood Knocks: A Journal of Sasquatch Research
Volume One
Volume Two
Volume Three
Volume Four
Volume Five

Table of Contents

1
Foreword

5
Introduction

PART ONE:
Water Creatures and Flying Monsters

11
Iowa Water Monsters

23
Raccoon River Monster

25
Modern Accounts

29
The Skunk River Monster Tale

35
Monsters in the Air

39
The Van Meter Visitor

49
The Aftermath

55
The Mystery of the Plaster Cast

59
The Visitor Lingers

PART TWO:
Bigfoot in Iowa

67
Bigfoot in the Hawkeye State

71
Wild Men

77
Early Accounts

87
The Lockridge Monster

95
The Ottosen Creature

105
Bigfoot Through the Decades

PART THREE:
Weird Things in the Hawkeye State

149
Curious Beasts

153
Unusual Swine

157
Phantom Kangaroos

159
A Menagerie of Big Cats

173
Giant Snakes

185
Humanoid Monsters

187
Giants

193
Iowa Vampire

197
Werewolves

203
Weird Humanoids

213
Acknowledgements

215
Bibliography

219
Photo Credits

221
About the Author

MONSTERS OF THE HAWKEYE STATE by David Weatherly

Foreword

I have a confession: I used to think Iowa was a rather boring state. From the outside, I thought the Hawkeye state was only known for cornfields, the birthplace of sliced bread, and the famous Grant Wood painting *American Gothic*, with its stiffly posed farmer and his daughter standing in front of a Carpenter Gothic farmhouse with pitchfork in hand. Not exactly big selling points for tourism or adventure. This is a state that has more pigs than people—8 to 1, in fact. That said, the more time I spent in Iowa the more I realized my previous assumptions were very naïve. I couldn't have been more wrong. You need the eyes of a hawk to discover all the mysteries and rich Iowan folklore hidden just under the surface. Maybe that's the real reason it's called the Hawkeye state. It's here—lots of it—you just have to know where to look. And let me tell you; David Weatherly found them—he has the eye.

When David told me he was doing a book on Iowa creatures I was a little concerned. I knew he could do it, but it probably wouldn't be an easy book to write. Damned hard was more likely. I thought he might get the 'holler tail' over it. That's an old Iowa farm phrase for when someone's in a terrible mood. You see, unlike some other states, Iowans keep their legends and secrets close to their chest. If one tries to discuss ghosts and strange beasts, they'll find people are rather reserved and tight-lipped. Until relatively recently people didn't discuss, let alone celebrate, their local monsters. I assume this is partly born of general Midwestern skepticism and perhaps fear of ridicule. Fortunately, that has all begun to change. Remember: the best way to keep unique local legends alive and prevent them from vanishing from history is by talking about them. Stories and folklore are a fascinating part of Hawkeye heritage, so keep those wild tavern tales and creepy campfire stories alive.

1

I knew the difficulties of Iowa research all too well. In 2011 I began a research project on an obscure hundred-year-old Iowan legend that was nearly forgotten. I, along with fellow researchers Chad Lewis and Noah Voss, discovered a wild story originating out of a small Iowa town called Van Meter, located just west of Des Moines. Back in 1903 the town was terrorized for five straight nights by a huge bat-winged creature. According to reports, it had a horn on its head that projected a bright beam of light. The creature also emitted a terrible odor that caused some to feel faint or nauseated. Townsfolk shot at it on numerous occasions, but incredibly it seemed impervious to gunfire. Finally, they traced it to an abandoned mine on the edge of town where they believed it had taken up roost. It was an amazing tale. You'll get the full story later in this book. The deeper we dug, the more details we found regarding the incident. Much more—enough to fill a book. We realized this near-vanished episode of Iowan history was simply too interesting and unique to let fade away like the old brittle newspaper clippings we'd found. The end result was our book, *The Van Meter Visitor: A True and Mysterious Encounter with the Unknown*.

During our project's deep dive into Iowan lore, we quickly realized Iowa is FULL of eerie tales, strange encounters, and mysterious locations. My opinion of the state was forever changed, and now Iowa holds a special fascination for me. In fact, the allure was so powerful that I now call it home. I couldn't resist buying a spooky 1887 Carpenter Gothic house in northeast Iowa (ironically the same rare style featured in Iowa's famous and aforementioned *American Gothic* painting). It has been a strange and unexpected journey over the last decade. Whether it's western Iowa's eerie wind-swept prairies or the archaic steamboat towns along the Mississippi River Valley, eventually Iowa works its way into your bones. Of course, this is nothing new to longtime residents, but for those unfamiliar with the region, this book is bound to spark your imagination and awaken interest in an oft-overlooked part of the country. And maybe, like me, you'll hear that siren's call and choose to stay.

When David approached me to contribute to this book,

I was thrilled to be part of something so close to my heart and also very excited that readers will finally get a peek into some previously unexamined Iowa-style oddities. Everyone knows about other famous American monsters like the Jersey Devil or West Virginia's Mothman, but Iowa's legends and monsters are virtually unknown—even within the state! This is uncharted territory. You won't find many of these cases and reports published anywhere else. Here you will discover creatures like the Lockridge Monster and the Ottosen Creature. It's great to see so many of these little-known stories gathered together for the first time and rescued from obscurity—an amazing feat, and I'm sure David would agree that it wasn't an easy task.

After reading the other volumes comprising his Monsters of America series, I had no doubt David was the perfect man for the job. I knew he wasn't afraid of 'going gravel' for a good story. That's an Iowa saying for getting off the beaten track and hitting the back country roads (which are often dirt and gravel around here). Who knows, maybe this book will inspire some readers into 'going gravel' themselves to find some of the sites mentioned in this book. Or perhaps embolden them to come forth with their own stories and experiences, further enriching Iowa's legends and lore.

Kevin Lee Nelson
—Always ready to go gravel in his black Dodge Charger.

Introduction

Iowa, known as the Hawkeye State, is part of the American Midwest. Tucked into the middle of the country, it shares a border with six other states—Illinois, Minnesota, Missouri, Nebraska, South Dakota, and Wisconsin.

Mention the state of Iowa, and most people will likely think of vast fields of farmland, prairie, and grasslands and corn. Lots and lots of corn. There's a good reason for this, Iowa is part of the United States Corn Belt, a region that has dominated the country's corn production since the 1850s.

Native tribes who once dominated the state include the Ioway, the Sac & Fox, and the Sioux.

Europeans first explored the land in the 1670s when Jacques Marquette and Louis Joliet arrived. The land was claimed by the French and remained their territory until 1762 when it was transferred to the Spanish who controlled it until 1800. The land eventually became part of Louisiana Territory, a huge tract of land that was obtained by the United States as part of the Louisiana Purchase in 1803. The purchase practically doubled the size of the US and Iowa was one of the states that eventually emerged from the deal. First designated as Iowa Territory, Iowa became a state and was admitted to the Union in 1846.

During the American Civil War, Iowa joined the Union side of the conflict and contributed fighting men to the Northern forces.

USA Today newspaper named Iowa the "most American state" due in part to several things that are considered all-American. Notably, aside from its vast farmland, Iowa has the highest number of bald eagles per square mile, has produced the most astronauts and the most Major League baseball players per capita, and Iowa natives have won more Olympic gold medals per capita than any other state.

Additionally, Iowa is rated overall one of the safest states in the country, a fact some attribute to gun ownership—the state has the largest percentage of homes with firearms.

Famous people born in the Hawkeye State include western icon William Fredrick "Buffalo Bill" Cody, western movie icon John Wayne (born Marion Morrison), actors Gene Wilder and Elija Wood, talk show host Johnny Carson and American big band leader Glenn Miller.

In addition, you can also thank Iowa for sliced bread—Otto Rohwedder, the man who invented the bread slicing machine—was born in the state.

One other notable figure connected to Iowa is the fictional Captain of the Starship Enterprise—James T. Kirk. Kirk is an Iowa native, or at least, he will be when he's born in 2228. The franchise's massive fan following led to a monument being placed in the town of Riverside noting it as the captain's future birthplace. It's both a curious attraction and a testament to the enduring popularity of Star Trek.

Iowa is ranked the 31st most populous state and comes in at number 26 in land area. Des Moines is both the state capital and the largest city.

Manufacturing and biotechnology are both big contributors to Iowa's economy and, of course, so is agriculture which started booming in the state in the early 1900s and remains an economic cornerstone. It was agriculture, specifically, the advent of large-scale farming, that drastically transformed Iowa's landscape.

Today, less than one percent of the tallgrass prairie that once covered much of the state remains intact. Crops now cover about sixty percent of the land. Lost, too, is most of the state's original forest—only about seven percent of Iowa is forested. The remaining percentages include urban areas, and remaining grasslands, prairie, and wetlands.

The Hawkeye State has a wide range of wildlife including white-tail deer, red and gray fox, bobcat, otters, opossums, muskrat, chipmunk, and coyote.

Moose and mountain lions are occasionally reported in Iowa, though officials say the animals are not resident species, but merely passing through from neighboring states.

Bird species include the brightly colored American goldfinch (the state bird), the bobolink, the blue-winged teal, swans, cranes, and many other species.

Catfish, walleye, and crappie are among the fish that populate the state's waters, and there are plenty of other aquatic species to boot.

Then, there are the other, unofficial creatures that are found in Iowa. While many believe there's not enough cover in the state to hide the hairy biped known as Bigfoot, the creatures themselves didn't get the memo. Sightings of the beast tend to cluster around Iowa's waterways and reported encounters stretch back for many years.

Big cats are also reported in the state, some of the infamous black panther variety. Oddly, there are also accounts of "sea serpents," the last thing one would expect in a landlocked, Midwestern state.

What may be more unnerving for many are the giant snake reports that have come from the state.

The state's most notable and unique cryptid is the Van Meter Visitor, a strange, flying…something that rocked a small town in the early 1900s. Does it still lurk somewhere in the Hawkeye State?

Sit back and dive in for an exploration of the Monsters of the Hawkeye State.

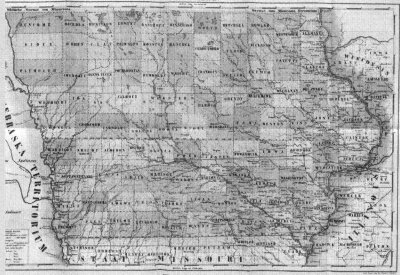

Karte des Staates **IOWA**

nach den besten Hülfsmitteln bearbeitet von

Th. Olshausen.

PART ONE
Water Creatures and Flying Monsters

Iowa Water Monsters

Some may be shocked to learn that Iowa has reports of water monsters. Even though the state doesn't have a coastline, it does have plenty of fresh water, including a group of natural lakes known as the Iowa Great Lakes. This group of seven bodies of water is in the northwestern portion of the state. The largest of the seven is Spirit Lake which stretches over 5,684 acres. The East and West Okoboji lakes are also part of the Iowa Great Lakes.

According to legend, the lakes are connected to the Gulf of Mexico via a large, underground river. Some people suggest that such a connection to the open ocean allows strange and unknown creatures a path to the state's lakes, a connection that has allowed sea serpents to visit the region.

In addition to numerous other, smaller lakes, several major rivers flow through Iowa, including the mighty Mississippi River, the Missouri River, the Des Moines River, and the Big Sioux River.

In terms of water monster lore, reportedly, there is, or was, a monster turtle in a pond in Cerro Gordo County. The Big Blue Pond in Lester Milligan Park, Mason City, is the creature's lair, and it's supposed to be as large as the hood of a Volkswagen.

The thirty-four-foot-deep pond is a popular spot for outdoor recreation and is a gathering spot for both local and national divers.

Tales of the pond's turtle have circulated for some time, though eyewitness accounts are difficult to come by. On his *Cryptozoonews* blog, Loren Coleman provides comments about the turtle from Jim Wahl, a fisheries management biologist with the Iowa Department of Natural Resources at Clear Lake. Wahl states:

"I've heard rumors that there's one [a turtle] as big as the hood of a Volkswagen, but I don't believe it. The rumors I hear come through third, fourth-hand, scuba-diving sightings. Whether it's legitimate or not, I don't know."

Most of the stories of the creature do seem to come from scuba divers, but as Wahl notes, it's difficult to find actual witnesses who say they've seen the animal.

Some people believe the animal is a normal snapping turtle while others argue that the species isn't present in Iowa.

Wahl expressed further doubt of a turtle being in the pond, saying that the spot "is not a monster's kind of hangout: snappers prefer small streams, creeks, marshes and shallow lakes."

Being a biologist at Clear Lake, Wahl would probably have quite a laugh if he heard about a 1914 report from the lake involving a "human appearing fish."

According to a report in Marshalltown, Iowa's *Evening Times-Republican* on June 29, 1914, residents around Clear Lake said a weird fish person was stealing food from the wharves on a nightly basis:

"Night Vigil of Resorters Fails to Solve Mystery—

"Clear Lake, June 29—What has been termed by the summer colony as the 'Human Fish' has been discovered on the north shore of Clear Lake and is causing more excitement than has prevailed at this summer resort for a number of years. The discovery of the strange phenomenon was brought about by cottagers who had food taken off their piers which run into the lake and the statement of a number who declare they have seen the strange creature.

"Several parties have gone out in an effort to catch the mysterious visitor, but each effort has been, up to date, without result.

"A few nights ago, a party of guests at the Oaks Hotel went down to the lake beach and started an all-night vigil in an effort to capture it. Just at midnight when the lights went out about the pier, a ripple in the water was seen and a human arm was extended out of the water. It grabbed some food which had been placed on the end of the pier and was again withdrawn into the water. The watchers rushed to the pier end, but they saw nothing. However, a dark spot a ways out in the lake near 100 yards away was seen hurrying thru the water and a weird laugh was heard rippling over the water.

"Some fishermen who were out in a boat last Thursday claim to have seen what they took to be a man swimming with fish-like speed thru the water. They gave chase in their boat but as they neared the man or animal, it dove, and a similar laughter was heard from the rushes which were about fifty yards away.

"Sea Monster or Man?

"It is believed that the strange inhabitant of the lake is either a sea monster which has by some method found a home in the lake or else is a demented man whose love for swimming has caused him to spend most of his time in the water, getting his food from the piers and cottages and sleeping like Moses of old, in the bull rushes along the lake's shore. The proximity of the county home between Clear Lake and Mason City where a number of unfortunates are housed led to an investigation and it was found that there are none of the inmates missing. Instead of solving the mystery the solutions seemed farther away.

"Hunting the human fish has become a pastime with the colonists. The description given by those who claim to have seen it describe it as a small sized man about 50 years of age and whose body seems to be covered with scales like a fish, caused perhaps by the roughening of his skin by constant staying in the water. Others claim it is impossible for the creature to be a man because of the long time it stays under water. However, every effort is being made to solve the mystery and motor launch loads of people can be seen daily skirting the lake looking for the strange creature whose mysterious visits have so aroused the summer colony."

Des Moines River, Humboldt County

The weird human-fish man wasn't the earliest report of aquatic oddities in Iowa. In its August 13, 1885, edition, Humeston, Iowa's paper the *Humeston New Era*, reported that a sea serpent was active in the Des Moines River. Apparently, it had been spotted previously though no details of the previous encounters were provided. The paper reported:

"The Des Moines River sea serpent has been seen again, this time near Durham, Marion County. One Daniel Morgan saw it and shot at it twice, but without effect. It was 12 feet long, as thick around as the body of a man, and had a horn on its head a foot long."

The story is of course doubtful and further confused when we note that the article was reprinted from an undated edition of the *Ottumwa Courier* and was related to that paper by a correspondent from the *Knoxville Express*. It seems the *Muscatine Daily Journal* had reported the same story a week previous in its August 7, 1885, edition, without the witness's name or the detail that the man had shot at the creature.

All in all, it makes the story sound like a strange game of telephone involving a sea serpent in an Iowa river. Maybe it was inspired by some real encounter, but if so, the true tale is well obscured at this point.

Another case with more details comes from the summer of 1886 when a water monster frightened a pair of mill workers in Muscatine County. According to the June 9 report in Muscatine's *Daily Journal*, the creature was living in the Mississippi River. The paper said that news of the monster had gotten out and was causing great concern:

"It has not been generally known uptown, but it has got out to some alarming extent among the moonlight skiff parties of ladies and gentlemen who are in the habit of enjoying their evenings on the river that a terrible serpent of sufficient coil to play havoc with a whole pleasure fleet, has recently been seen in our waters. In the various stories told of this strange visitor he has been made to assume every form imaginable, from the regular sea serpent to the hideous devil fish and other monstrous creatures of the deep, until these exaggerations have tended to make one believe that the horrid thing was a creature of pure fiction."

To ensure that the creature was not a fabrication, the paper sent a reporter to South Muscatine to interview two mill workers who said they had encountered the beast.

Henry Judisch, 21, and Willie Bloom, 15, were employees of the Hershey upper mill and were vouched for by their foreman Gen. Banks as "truthful and sober-minded" individuals. The two men were interviewed separately, and their stories matched. They had encountered the creature the previous week on one of their days off from the mill. The article reports:

"The young men rowed a skiff over to the Illinois shore toward evening to engage in fishing. They reached a point opposite the Towhead and, hauling their boat ashore, were sitting down arranging their lines and bait, when young Bloom caught sight of the serpent, but a little ways from shore, coming down stream! The head of the snake was poised over a foot above water, and its body was visible in curves for ten or twelve feet behind. The head was about the size of a man's double fist, and Judisch describes it as looking like a blue racer's. Its head turned from side to side, sometimes with open mouth, and the boys say that it made a head ripple and swell in the water as it moved along, like the passing of a skiff."

15

Judisch estimated the serpent was about 20 to 30 feet from the shore. The sight of the creature frightened Bloom so much that he ducked down and hid behind the boat shaking with fear.

The creature passed back and forth several times before turning and making a run toward the two men on shore. At this, the men fled. As the *Journal* reports:

"They shoved that skiff off shore quicker than a boat was ever launched before, and seizing the oars, made swift work for home. Judisch says he has had enough fishing over there for a spell, and a free pass to Saturday's circus wouldn't begin to hire young Bloom to take a skiff across the river. Each says it was plain daylight and that the serpent was as visible in its neck and head and rolling body, as if it had lain at their feet."

If the story has any truth to it, I question why the two men felt like it was a good idea to get into the water where the creature was to begin with rather than running further ashore.

Not only had sea serpents made their way inland to Iowa's lakes and rivers, but they also even turned up in ponds. The *Iowa State Reporter* mentioned a Butler County water monster in its May 24, 1888, edition, reporting:

"In the Clarksville Mill Pond there is a strange reptile, which the *Star* believes to be a sea serpent. It is a strange beast that eats babies and has whiskers."

As frightening as the creature sounds, it didn't get any more attention in the news. It's somewhat surprising since many newspapers of the period liked to expound on tales of bizarre creatures. Of course, they weren't always strictly fanciful stories. Sometimes odd accounts were explained. Take the case involving a weird something that showed up in the town of Independence in Buchanan County.

The September 4, 1890, edition of *Forest and Stream* reported on a nocturnal monster that had shown up around the town and was causing a stir among the locals. Residents of the Kress neighborhood said the creature was "making the night hideous with its roaring." Reportedly, the animal's cries sounded like "a cross between the roar of a lion and the screech of an enraged panther."

The animal was purportedly an aquatic beast that had taken up residence in a nearby creek. No one seemed to know where the thing had come from.

People in the area were working themselves up in a panic, no doubt imagining all kinds of dreadful beasts lurking in the night, but in this case, the mystery was soon solved. The "monster" turned out to be a blind mule that had gotten lost. It's braying noises were apparently the terrifying sound that locals were hearing at night.

In the summer of 1903, a "mammoth creature" was spotted in the East Okoboji Lake. Estherville, Iowa's *Vindicator & Republican* reported on the thing in its July 3 edition, questioning whether or not the creature was a sea serpent:

"Nearly every fashionable resort has one, then why should not Okoboji be the possessor of one?

"One thing is certain, and that is that some unknown creature is alive in the waters of that lake, that would undoubtedly hurry a good husky person to land with hook and line."

The paper recounted an incident involving Mr. and Mrs. Charles Bartlett who were on the lake fishing when they spotted something very large in the water.

"They have no idea what it was," the paper reported, "it might have been a sea serpent, or it might have been some kind of a fish that had grown to unusual and extraordinary size."

The couple were out in their boat when they noticed a "terrible commotion" in the lake. They next saw a massive object moving rapidly through the water. The creature was near the surface and its movement made waves so large that Mr. Bartlett was worried that his boat would be swamped with water.

The witnesses said the thing looked like an overturned skiff, but the nature of its movements indicated that it was a living creature. According to the paper, Bartlett "would not have believed there was such a creature in the lake had he not seen with his own eyes the commotion made by it."

The same year, on August 10, the *Janesville Daily Gazette* reported that a nine-foot-long alligator had been found near the town of Clinton, Clinton County. According to the report, a man named Charles Laing shot and killed the gator in the Mississippi River, noting that it was the first one ever seen in the area.

In its February 11, 1904, edition, Muscatine's *Journal* announced that a sea lion was spotted around Towhead Island, a small piece of land in the Mississippi River.

Railroad men were the first to spot the creature out on the ice. At first, the large animal was mistaken for a drowning horse. The paper reports:

"Tuesday evening, the brakeman of extra No. 246, of the Rock Island, while passing the old Hershey Mill, saw what he thought to be a horse drowning in the air hole above Towhead Island. He quickly called the attention of his companions to it. They watched it as long as the place was in sight. The last thing they saw was a great beast apparently in its death struggles in the icy water. Then all was still and not a splash agitated the surface of the water. Then suddenly a great form shot high in the air and fell with a resounding splash in the water. The brakemen looked at each other and remarked that the horse had died hard."

The animal hadn't perished, however, and it was soon spotted again. The day after the railroad men saw the creature, a man and his wife traveling from South Muscatine spotted it at the same location. Their attention was first attracted to a commotion in the water around the air hole. The *Journal* reported:

"They stopped, thinking someone had fallen in the water and was drowning. They were astonished beyond measure to see the form of a strange beast crawl out on the ice and lie still. Observing this they hastened up town and told several people who were congregated at the fish market about the strange happening. A powerful telescope was brought to bear upon the spot indicated and there, stretched in the sun, lay the form of what appeared to be a sea lion. Keeping the animal covered with the telescope a number of the party started down on the ice towards the animal. When the men had traversed about half the distance the form was seen to slip into the water and disappear.

"Upon arriving at the air hole, the investigating party found the ice covered with water splashed over the surface and in several places, wet spots were noticed on the surface of the ice, presumably made by the beast when lying down. Nothing more was seen of the animal."

The *Journal* also noted that workers at a sawmill on the Illinois side of the river had reported seeing a strange animal in the water around the same location.

Various locals tried to devise a plan to catch the animal, but since it was near impossible to get close to it, no one was sure how to capture it. The paper also stated that the animal was likely an escaped sea lion:

"The only known escaped sea lion is 'Big Ben,' who escaped from the Lincoln Park Zoo a few months ago. This animal was an exceedingly large one and weighed in the neighborhood of 800 pounds. A clam digger at work on the ice between the dams above the city was frightened nearly out of his wits recently by the appearance of a strange animal in the water of the air hole where he was at work. It would not be an impossibility for the animal to have made the trip, coming down the Chicago drainage canal and from there up the river."

The paper never explained how the sea lion had escaped from the zoo to begin with, if indeed that's what the animal was. Developments were being "watched with interest" but nothing more seems to have come of the story.

Iowa Water Monsters

MONSTERS OF THE HAWKEYE STATE by David Weatherly

Raccoon River Monster

Local legend says that a monster once lived in the Raccoon River in Dallas County between the towns of Van Meter and Wiscotta.

Some say the creature looked like a cross between a turtle and a seal. Obviously, such a combination is impossible, but witnesses who spotted it in years past claimed the beast had a hard shell like a turtle, and that it moved using its seal-like flippers.

Lori Pielak spoke to one man who spent his life living near the river. He called the creature Jezabel, or Jezy for short. In her book, *Ghosts of Dallas County*, Pielak writes that the man, Abe Johnson, told her that the creature appeared in the area every few years. It would linger for a brief time before departing the area until its next visit. He claimed to have first seen the monster when he was six years old, but when asked if it still visited, he told Pielak that it had not been seen in twenty-eight years.

"I think she's no longer with us," he said. "At least not in the physical. Jezy will always be a part of the Raccoon River whether anyone wants to believe or not."

Pielak also heard a story about a father and son who saw the creature. They described it as eight feet in length with a tail like a fish, a hard-shelled body like a turtle, a head and neck that extended out, and flippers.

Few locals talk about the water monster anymore, so it seems it is a legend that is fading away with time.

Modern Accounts

In modern times, there have been far fewer water monster reports in the state.

On August 3, 1941, the *United Press* reported that a "man-eating catfish" was attacking people near Hayward's Bay on West Okoboji Lake. According to the report a man was knocked down by a blow from the creature and both he and a woman were wounded by the fish.

The article mentions that several years previous "a 20-pound belligerent catfish was seined out of Spirit Lake after it had attacked several people."

Officials from the state's fisheries department were planning to use the same process to catch the catfish harassing people at West Okoboji Lake.

Jumping well forward, there were a few accounts of something strange in West Okoboji Lake in the early 2000s. Michael Newton's *Encyclopedia of Cryptozoology* lists a June 23, 2001, encounter. According to the listing, three witnesses saw a lake monster rise out of the water and scrape against the dock that they were standing on. One of those present said the creature's head was a "very good-sized oval or sphere" and was larger than a bowling ball. The beast was dark green or blue and no scales were visible.

In recent years, locals have reported finding some piranha in the Missouri River on a couple of occasions. These are most certainly exotic pets that have been released into the wild.

Giant catfish have also been reported in several bodies of water in the state. It's well-known that the fish can be found in the Hawkeye State, but some witnesses claim there are specimens out there far bigger than any on record.

One interesting note about Iowa's water monsters—paddlefish used to live in the waters of both the East and West Okoboji Lakes. Mary Kennedy, curator of the Iowa Great Lakes Maritime Museum, reports that the largest paddlefish caught in the area weighed 210 pounds and measured six and a half feet long. It was caught in 1919 and is commonly noted as the last one caught in the Okoboji. A replica of the fish is on display at the museum.

The fish used to make their way into the lakes from the Missouri River via the Little Sioux River. Kennedy notes that when dam construction began at the outlet of Lower Gar Lake, the paddlefish were cut off and could no longer make their way into the Okoboji. The last survivors were eventually caught or died off. At least, officially that is. It's possible that some paddlefish survived longer and if so, it could explain some later lake monster sightings at Okoboji, especially older accounts.

The fish are unusual looking, especially for those unfamiliar with the species. They area slate gray in color, have an extremely long snout, long gill covers, and a mouth similar to a shark. When paddlefish are young, they have small, fine teeth which eventually fall out as they age.

They may look and sound vicious, but paddlefish survive on a diet of plankton and small water plants and are harmless to humans.

The Skunk River

The Skunk River Monster Tale

One of Iowa's more outrageous monster tales chronicles the purported struggle to bring down a massive water monster that was in the Skunk River in the late 1800s.

There's really no doubt the story is a fabrication and was likely the product of Al Swalm who not only ran a local newspaper but was also known in the area as a prankster.

I include the complete original tale here for historical purposes for those interested in the folklore of monsters. The account below was published in the January 8, 1885, edition of the Ligonier Leader.

"A Huge Monster"

"A Huge River Reptile or Animal Captured in the Skunk River near Oskaloosa, Iowa"

"The wildest excitement ever known in Iowa, amounting almost to frenzy, now prevails at Skunk River near Oskaloosa. The excitement began Tuesday, and though somewhat abated, still exists, and there are now several hundred persons there and many others hurrying to the scene. Early Tuesday morning Mr. James Wright, living a few miles from Oskaloosa, rode into town and informed the city authorities of what he had seen at his farm. His statements are as follows:

"His farm is situated four or five miles from the city, on the south bank of the river. His feed lot, in which ten days ago there were about one hundred large hogs, is situated about eight rods at the nearest point to the river. During the last twenty days ten of his largest hogs, weighing from 250 to 400 pounds, have very mysteriously disappeared. The fence was new and made of native lumber, with posts every six feet; also, a trusty bulldog slept four rods from the lot, and there was no evidence that the fence had been touched or the dog aroused; the mystery surrounding the missing hogs was becoming darker each day. Last night he, armed with a Henry rifle and his dog by his side, from a partially concealed spot watched the pen or lot. Nothing whatever was seen during the night, and nothing heard except violent splashing in the river. Just as the sun rose, and he was in the act of starting home, there came from the river up over the bank, and slowly moving towards the hog lot, a gigantic animal or reptile, large enough and hideous enough to appall the strongest man. And had not subsequent measurements verified his estimate of size, length, etc., those having heard his excited statements would have still believed that his exaggerations resulted from fear. It approached the pen in which the hogs were kept more slowly than it emerged from the river and carried its head several feet above the fence until about fifteen or twenty feet of its head and body was beyond the fence when, with a quick descent of the head, a hog weighing at least 300 pounds was grasped in the mouth of the monster. The entire hog disappeared in the mouth, except the head, which projected out of the side of the animal's mouth about fifteen inches from the tip of the nose. It then turned around without seeming to move its hind legs or tail, carrying its head at least twelve or fifteen feet high, its fore legs not touching during the time it was getting over the fence. It then ran down the river bank fifteen or twenty rods and plunged into the water. He estimated its entire length to be 78 feet; the distance from the fore legs to the end of the nose at 18 feet; the distance between the fore legs and hind legs at 40 feet; and the tail at 20 feet. Its legs were 4 feet long and as thick as a man's body. Its body was from four to five feet in diameter, making the animal when walking about 7 or 8 feet high.

Although no one believed his statements accurately, all believed some wonderful animal had been seen and that it had carried a large hog into the river. The report spread rapidly and in one hour forty or fifty men on horseback and several hundred on foot were hurrying to the Wright farm. The animal was first seen a mile below the farm. Several shots were fired into him which produced no other effect than to cause him to approach the bank slowly and unexcitedly, but when within ten or fifteen feet of the bank suddenly made a lunge and grasped by the head and neck a horse ridden by Wm. Smith, and was jerked with such force as to carry him into the river, and so deep did his teeth go that his flesh was mangled and the neck bone exposed in many places back to the body. Wm. T. Smith was only saved from being carried in with the horse by being caught by the arm and held by John Aikin, who was riding near him. The animal then plunged into the middle of the river, and it was apparent from the commotion in the water (and his body was seen every few rods) that he was going down stream rapidly. Every man with gun or revolver at every opportunity fired at him. The number increased so that at twelve o'clock there were two thousand following his movements. The firing along the bank became so frequent and reckless, or perhaps thoughtless, that it seemed like a battle field. Neither the roar of the musketry nor the impact of the bullets against his body seemed to disturb him.

"By this time, it became apparent that revolver and rifle ball would not penetrate his body, as it was roughly estimated that up to 3 p.m., ten thousand shots had been fired, without even having infuriated him. At this time Al. Swalm, of Oskaloosa, directed two men to make the best possible time to town and bring a 12-pound cannon, a keg of railroad spikes and plenty of powder. The cannon arrived at 4 p.m. Capt. Wilber, who commanded the 23rd Indiana battery through the Atlanta campaign, took command of the gun. It was heavily loaded with powder and railroad spikes and put in position covering the river at a shoal a half mile below, and all waited impatiently the result. At twenty minutes past five the huge river reptile exposed a large portion of his body in crossing the shoal, when at a distance of 38 feet the cannon was fired. Even before the roar of the cannon had died away in the distance, a piteous wail, or groan, loud and long, came from the water; the head and tail lashed the water furiously; the water near the middle of the animal was seen to be deeply tinged with blood. In a few minutes all motion had ceased, and it could be seen that the railroad spikes had taken effect just behind the fore leg, and that a large stream of blood gushed from the wound. A ditching team, consisting of 12 yoke of oxen, were a mile distant. They were brought, and chains were thrown about its head, and it was drawn upon the river bank. Al. Swalm and Dr. Huntsman made accurate measurements, which are as follows: Entire length from end of tail to tip of nose 81 feet; from the fore legs to tip of nose, 21 feet; body, from fore to hind legs, 40 feet; its tail 20 feet. Its heart weighed 80 pounds and had four cavities and was pronounced by Huntsman to be the heart of an air breathing animal, and not a reptile. The lungs and all other organs seemed like the viscera of animals. It was found that not one of the bullets had penetrated the skin.

"It was skinned, and a taxidermist is employed to stuff it, and it will be sent to the Academy of National Science, at Philadelphia. The flesh is being carefully removed from its skeleton, which is to be properly wired and kept for the present at Oskaloosa on exhibition.

"Dr. Peck of Davenport arrived in response to a telegram Wednesday morning. After a very careful examination he said: 'Gentlemen, this is no Cardiff giant, but a veritable animal or reptile, but as I am neither a naturalist or paleontologist, I have only to say that it probably belongs to a species of gigantic lizard supposed to have been extinct many thousands of years.' Pointing to one of the teeth he said: 'I will give fifty dollars for that canine tooth,' which was found on measurement to be seventeen and a half inches long."

Monsters in the Air

Several years ago, I was asking some Iowa residents about a purported thunderbird (giant bird) sighting in the state. The priceless response from one old farmer was: "I got too much work to do to be staring off into the skies."

Obviously, the comment doesn't apply to everyone, but it was an interesting commentary on the work ethic of many residents in the state's vast farmland regions. Taken at face value, the comment is something to consider when we note that there's not a big catalog of flying creature accounts in the state.

Ultimately, I found out very little about the purported thunderbird since it was, sadly, a case of a "friend of a friend" reporting the incident.

Author Brad Steiger collected an interesting giant bird story, detailed in his book *Real Monsters, Gruesome Critters, and Beasts from the Darkside*. Brad received the account via personal correspondence with a man named Tim from Clinton County.

Tim told Steiger that in 1986, he was out hunting when he spotted a massive bird that stood over six feet tall. The bird was bronze and black in color and was sitting on a tree branch. Tim said the creature looked somewhat like an eagle, though much larger in size.

A few nights after seeing the bird, Tim attended a campground lecture about birds of prey in the region. He told Steiger:

"I described the giant bird in detail for the biologist, but the scientist told me that such a bird was impossible. There were no birds in the Americas larger than a condor, and there were no condors in Iowa."

Another weird flying creature dates back much further,

specifically, to 1887. The August 11 edition of Bedford, Iowa's *Times-Independent*, reported on a "flying serpent" seen over the town by a man named Lee Corder. The paper reports:

"Mr. Corder says when first seen it resembled a buzzard, but as it drew nearer its appearance was different from any flying animal he had ever seen. As it descended lower and its outline became more distinct, it took the form of a great serpent, writhing and twisting. With protruding eyes and forked tongue, great scales, which glistened in the sunlight, covered its huge body, which appeared to be flat and nearly a foot in width. While they were gazing at it with awe and astonishment, it landed in a cornfield, a few rods distant, with a dull thud. Those who saw it were so frightened that they did not dare to go to the field in search of it, and it was allowed to pass on its way unmolested. Many theories have been advocated as to the probable nativity of the insect, but none appear plausible."

The *Times* assured its readers of the "unimpeachable veracity" of Lee Corder and his family and suggested that anyone who doubted the tale could pay them a visit to hear the story themselves.

Despite the small number of flying cryptid reports in Iowa, the state's most famous monster is, hands down, a winged thing that plagued a small town in the early 1900s, the infamous Van Meter Visitor.

Monsters in the Air

Van Meter Train Depot circa 1907

The Van Meter Visitor

Van Meter is a small town in Dallas County in central Iowa. The area was originally part of land belonging to the Sac and Fox tribes. White settlers started arriving in the 1840s and the area began to slowly grow. Brothers Daniel and Lewis Stump arrived in 1845 and realized the land was rich in resources, and more pioneers soon followed, adding to the then rough settlement community. The town started to form and was officially laid out in 1869. Originally called "Tracy," the town's name was changed to Van Meter in honor of early Dutch settler Jacob Rhodes Van Meter. The town of Van Meter was officially incorporated in 1877.

It's a quiet, friendly community and according to the 2020 census, the town has just under 1500 citizens.

Sports fans will note that Baseball Hall of Fame pitcher Bob Feller—known as the "hardest throwing pitcher of all time"—was born in Van Meter. The town has a display of Feller related memorabilia in City Hall to honor his legacy.

For those whose interest is geared toward things much stranger than the national pastime, the town is known for something else—the Van Meter Visitor—a bizarre creature that appeared from nowhere and briefly terrorized the town before vanishing and leaving an enduring mystery in its wake.

The tale of the visitor begins in 1903. A time when life was much simpler. Many citizens of Van Meter were farmers or small business owners while others were employed at the brick and tile factory just outside of town. None of them were prepared for the strange events that suddenly unfolded that fall. The story in the October 4, 1903, edition of the *Des Moines Daily News*, describes the scene:

"Quite frequently one hears of a haunted house, but for a whole town to have 'em' is a different proposition. Van Meter, a town of about 900 souls, lying 20 miles west of Des Moines, alone enjoys the distinction of being haunted. Queer noises are heard, hideous apparitions are seen, and uncanny lights move around in a mysterious manner."

While the opening of the paper's article may lead one to believe that a horde of poltergeist were at work, the strange events centered around a creature that suddenly appeared in town.

The strange events started on Monday night, September 28. Van Meter resident Ulysses G. Griffith was making his way home, unaware of what was about to unfold in the quiet town.

Ulysses and his brother were the owners of the Griffith Brothers Implement company, and Ulysses had spent the day making his rounds through the region selling tools and equipment to area farmers.

It was around one a.m. when Griffith finally made it back to Van Meter. No doubt he was looking forward to some well-deserved rest. Arriving in town, he quickly noticed something unusual—a bright light on the roof of Mather & Gregg's building downtown. Griffith had never seen the light before and as he continued toward it, he puzzled over what it was. His first thought was that it was some kind of electric spotlight, but that didn't seem to be the case. As he looked at the light, he became worried that burglars were at work. As he moved closer, he considered various explanations for the light. Before he could reach a conclusion, there was a dramatic change—the light suddenly moved across the street and settled on top of another building.

Before Griffith had time to further consider the source of the strange light, it vanished completely. Griffith continued home and turned in for the night, not realizing that he had been the first witness to a weird series of events that would rock the town.

The following day, the thirty-five-year-old Griffith told some townspeople about the light he had seen. Griffith was well respected in the community. A business owner, member of the Village Council and all-around balanced individual, there was no indication that he would fabricate the story for any reason. Griffith's account of the puzzling light was nothing compared to what was coming.

On Tuesday night, September 29, the town doctor, Dr. Alcott, was roused from his sleep by a bright light shining in his face. Alcott was sleeping in a room in the back of his office in town when the light woke him. The *Daily News* described Alcott's encounter with the source of the light:

"He is a plucky little fellow and grabbed his gun of immense proportions and ran outside the building, where he was confronted with something or other that seemed half human and half animal and yet had great bat-like wings, and the light seemed to come from a single blunt horn that grew out of its forehead."

Confronted by the bizarre sight, the good doctor brought his gun to bear on the creature. He was close and likely felt he couldn't miss his target. He started firing at the thing and let loose with five shots. None of them seem to affect the beast. With only one shot remaining, the doctor retreated back into his office. He barred the doors and windows and stayed inside until sunrise. The next day, he told his fellow citizens about the weird creature he had shot at the previous night. Combined with the account from Ulysses Griffith of the strange light moving across the rooftops, the townsfolk had to wonder exactly what was happening in their small community.

Events escalated rapidly. What had at first been a simple, unexplained light had now proven to be something altogether unknown—something living. Still, some people likely thought there was a rational explanation for the events, and some at least still thought that bandits were at work in town.

On Wednesday night, September 30, Clarence Dunn, known to his friends as Peter, was walking through town alone. Still a young man, Peter was already well respected in town. He was a cashier at the Van Meter Bank and had his sights set on higher positions. He would eventually achieve these, becoming bank manager and even town mayor. But on the night in question, Dunn was on his way to the bank to act as night watchman. He was armed with a shotgun and ready to settle in for the night. With the reports of the past two days, bank officials didn't want to take any chances since there could be robbers afoot.

Around one a.m., odd things began to occur. The town clock struck announcing the time and, along with it, Dunn heard another noise, one that wasn't familiar—a weird gasping as if someone, or something, was struggling for air. The odd noise was coming from the east side of the building. The man wasn't sure if the source was human or animal and before he could investigate the matter, a bright light shone through the front window of the bank. The light was so bright that Dunn was almost blinded by it. After shining on him a moment, the light moved, casting around the room as if looking for something. With the light no longer in his eyes, Dunn was able to get a look at the source of the illumination. A large form started to come into his view. Just as Dunn was starting to focus on it, the light hit him full in the face again, blinding him once more.

Between the tension and adrenaline of the moment, and the feeling of imminent danger, Dunn raised his gun and fired point blank at the large form outside the bank. The blasts from his gun shattered the window and part of the sash.

Dunn thought that he had killed the thing, but there was no sign of it. When morning broke, a thorough search was made of the area. The only indication that something had been there was a set of large, three toed tracks. According to the *Daily News*, Dunn made a plaster cast of one the prints, likely hoping it would aid in identifying the creature.

The following night, Thursday, October 1, another man—O. V. White—encountered the creature.

White was the co-owner of the Fisher & White Hardware and Furniture Store. He had second floor rooms over the hardware shop. Late that night he was roused from his sleep by a sound like that of "two rasps being rubbed together."

With gun in hand, White opened the window and peered outside. It was dark and rainy, and it took a few moments for his eyes to adjust, but he soon spotted what he thought was the source of the sound—a creature sitting on the cross arm of a nearby telephone pole. The thing may have been asleep or resting, and it was not emitting the light that other witnesses had reported. The paper describes the incident:

"Ordinarily Mr. White is a good shot, and he says he took deliberate aim and fired, but instead of killing it the shot only seemed to waken it up, and instantly its light was turned on him, and it emitted an odor that seemed to stupefy him, and he remembered no more about it."

Once again, a citizen had fired at close range and the creature remained unharmed. The strange odor that White reported was a new aspect though. The creature either had a naturally foul scent, or it emitted the odor as a skunk would.

Equally curious is the fact that White said he could not recall any of the night's events after he shot at the thing. Was the odor some kind of gas that affected his memory or perceptions?

Whatever the case, White was out of action, but another citizen was able to provide more details about the night's incident. The sound of White's gunfire had roused Sidney Gregg who was also sleeping in his store just across the corner from White's shop. Gregg leapt out of bed, armed himself, and rushed to the door to see what was happening.

Opening the front door, Gregg looked out and spotted the monster himself. It was descending the telephone pole as a parrot would, using its large beak to walk itself down. When the creature reached ground level, it stood upright and flapped its massive, featherless wings.

Gregg said the thing stood about eight feet tall and that the light emitting from its head was as bright as an electric headlight.

The man watched as the strange creature moved about like a kangaroo making great leaps. At times, it used its wings to assist its movements.

The Van Meter Visitor, art by Kevin Lee Nelson

Right on time, the local fast mail train came roaring down the tracks through town. The sound seemed to startle the beast, causing it to crouch as if it were about to spring up. According to the paper, the creature "ran on all four feet with wings extended and sailed away."

Gregg watched as the creature flew off toward the outskirts of town and the old coal mine. As the thing vanished in the night sky, the man finally remembered that he was holding a gun, one that he never even brought to bear while he was observing the beast.

The next sighting of the winged thing took place just outside of town. Late Friday night—the early hours of Saturday, October 3—J.L. Platt Jr. heard noises coming from the old mine shaft entrance. Platt was manager of the brick and tile factory

44

located on the same land where the old coal mine had been. Platt was likely familiar with the entrance since, according to a Dallas County census, he had been a director at the mine before it shut down.

At around one a.m., Platt heard unusual sounds coming from the mine shaft and went to investigate. According to news accounts, men at the brick factory had been hearing weird sounds come from the mine for some time.

The *Des Moines Daily News* (October 4, 1903), recounts the moment that Platt arrived at the shaft:

"The noise opened up again, as though Satan and a regiment of imps were coming forth for battle. But in a moment the monster appeared, accompanied by another somewhat smaller, but each gave off that brilliant light from the horn-like protuberance as they sailed away."

Now that the townspeople had discovered what appeared to be the monster's lair, they decided to take measures to end the creature. Electric lights were turned on all over town in an effort to keep the beasts at bay.

Armed men gathered to wait near the mine shaft, planning to ambush the creatures when they returned. For the rest of the night, the men sat and waited. Hours passed and there was still no sign of the monsters.

Around 5:45 in the morning the dawn began to break. The first rays of sunlight illuminated something else in the sky—the winged creatures, headed back to their lair after their nightly wanderings.

Guns blazed as the men opened fire, blasting at the beasts as the winged things shot towards the mine shaft. The foul odor, reported previously, was again emitted by the creatures. The monsters were unaffected by the onslaught of bullets. As the *News* reported:

"The reception they received would have sunk the Spanish fleet, but aside from unearthly noises and that peculiar odor, they did not seem to mind it, but slowly descended the shaft of the old mine."

Having failed in their attempts to kill the creatures, the townspeople decided to do the next best thing—barricade the mine entrance. The men set about the task with the obvious goal of finishing before nightfall when the monsters would again take to the sky.

On October 5, the *Des Moines Daily News* ran another brief item on the monster, but this one was more subdued and implied that the original story had been somewhat exaggerated. The paper reported:

"The 'mystery' that has served to considerably excite the residents is still unsolved. The account sent to newspapers by H.H. Phillips was, however, considerably exaggerated. The fact is that instead of there being some prehistoric or antediluvian monster living in this vicinity, there is either some very active practical joker or some energetic robber at large. It is true that divers [different] persons have been disturbed by various sounds and lights and that one bank official fired through the front of the building in a vain effort to hit some object that had awakened him by throwing a bright light through the window. Mr. Phillips has exercised his imagination to 'build up' a stronger story for newspaper publications, weaving fictitious details with the genuine."

Strangely, this is, for the most part, where the story ends. There was no follow-up report to verify whether the mine opening was covered before nightfall. Presumably, there were no further sightings of the creature that week since no further accounts were published.

VAN METER HOT UNDER THE COLLAR

TOWN HAS BEEN MALIGNED BY GHOST STORIES.

Citizens of the Place Feel Indignant Over the Matter, as It Gives the Place an Unenviable Reputation.

The town of Van Meter is justly indignant over a series of articles that have appeared in the Daily News, and the Capital is in receipt of a number of letters from citizens of that place who feel highly indignant over the matter. The articles alleged that the town was highly wrought up over the alleged affair. The principal article started out with the following:

"Quite frequently one hears of a haunted house, but for a whole town to have 'em is a different proposition. Van Meter, a town of about 200 souls, nine miles west of Des Moines, now enjoys the distinction of being haunted. Three people are said to have seen hideous apparitions of late and they behave in mysterious ways. . .

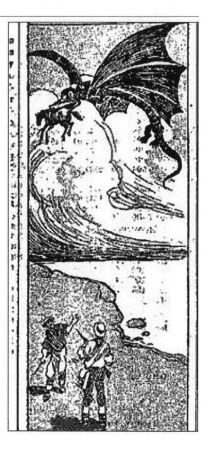

The Aftermath

In the following days after the last sighting, and well into November, other newspapers around the country ran stories about Van Meter's weird visitor. Some of these accounts contain inaccurate details about the events, notably, some witness names are altered or misrepresented. For instance, hardware store owner O.V. White was referred to as a doctor, clearly muddling him with Dr. Alcott. Alcott himself was at times listed as "Olcott." Such confusions can be understood given the time period of the events, but they can be distracting when one tries to get to the bottom of a mystery like the Van Meter Monster. It's important to look at the sources closest to the events and move forward from there, but even this is challenging in the case of the visitor because there just aren't many original articles to refer to.

One puzzling fact that I noticed during my research of the case involved the population of Van Meter. According to the official United States records from the time, the town had a population of around 400 citizens. News stories about the visitor, however, indicated a much large populace—around 1,000 people. This is a significant difference and it's not clear why there is such a large discrepancy. It's possible that official numbers didn't account for people living in the country around Van Meter, but even adding them to the total, it's unlikely the number would reach the one thousand mark. Most likely, the exaggerated number was a result of news writers estimating the population. Obviously, it's more dramatic to proclaim that a thousand people were being terrorized by some bizarre creature rather than a mere four hundred citizens. Remember, news sources tried to emphasize how frightening the situation was. As the October 11, 1903, edition of the *Saint Paul Globe* reported:

"The town of Van Meter, containing 1,000 persons, is terribly wrought up by what is described as a horrible monster. Every man, woman, and child in the town is in a state of terror, and fully half of them fail to close their eyes in slumber except in broad daylight."

Population numbers are important in cases like this for several reasons. A town with one thousand people would be expected to yield more eyewitnesses, but a town of a much smaller number would not.

The visitor may (or may not) have left town after the startling events of 1903, but it left behind a number of mysteries, foremost of which is—what was it?

Based on eyewitness descriptions of the winged beast, Professor Martin of Van Meter's South Side High School declared the creature "some sort of antediluvian monster." The statement conjures images of some terrible, ancient creature, roused from its slumber to torment the small Iowa town.

The implication is understandable. From descriptions of the thing, it matched no known creature. Other than the professor, we don't really know what citizens of Van Meter believed they were dealing with, but it seems that they, too, knew the visitor was something unnatural.

The skeptical minded have tried to point to the description of "bat-like wings" and claim that witnesses had seen a bat and, for some reason, became hysterical. This theory is easy to dismiss—you'll pardon the pun—right off the bat. According to the National Wildlife Federation, the largest bat found in the United States is the greater mastiff bat which comes in at seven inches in body length with a wingspan of up to 23 inches. This is a far cry from the massive size of Van Meter's monster. To top it off, there are no known bat species that have a horned head with light projection abilities!

In fact, the strange light that the Van Meter Visitor utilized during its time in town serves to eliminate any natural, known animal explanations. Over the years, various authorities have suggested owls, herons, cranes, and other common flying creatures as potential identities of the visitor, but obviously, they too can be discarded as explanations.

Overall, the bizarre combination of abilities demonstrated by the creature make the case extremely puzzling and almost immediately eliminate any natural explanation. What living creature emits a bright light, a memory erasing scent, and is impervious to bullets?

There's no denying that creatures like the visitor are downright confounding and such cases are troubling for investigators who try to find explanations that fit the natural world.

So, if it wasn't a known animal, where does that leave us? Some people have tried to dismiss the entire case as a fabricated news story, hoax, or a case of mass hallucination, but none of these explanations can explain the series of events, and under close scrutiny, they simply don't hold up. My friend and colleague Chad Lewis explored numerous potential explanations for the 1903 events and he, too, was left puzzled. As he notes in *The Van Meter Visitor*:

"The problem was that no sooner had I constructed one explanation, when new evidence pushed it right back down and I was forced to start over once again. When all the dust was settled, I had acquired more questions than answers."

One of the more intriguing theories is that something, some unknown creature, was living deep in the abandoned coal mine. The possibility is certainly an interesting one. The abandoned coal mine is a maze of tunnels and shafts deep into the earth. Borehole shafts can easily drop hundreds of feet down and have numerous twists and turns. If the creatures were using the mine as their lair, they would have plenty of space. Since they were observed coming out of the old mine entrance, it does indicate that they were, at the least, utilizing it and perhaps nesting inside. Clearly there's an implication that the weird noises heard by workers at the brick factory were from the activity of the creatures as well.

This leaves us with a question—did blocking the entrance (if it was fully blocked) put an end to the things, or were they unfazed? The creatures may well have had other entry and exit points and continued their nightly flights, but if this is the case, why were they not reported again in the days following the initial reports.

One final possibility is that the Van Meter Visitor was something akin to the more famous Mothman of West Virginia. West Virginia's creature was one that skirted the edges of the real and supernatural world and may have been an omen of some kind, heralding events to come in the sleepy town of Point Pleasant.

We don't have startling events linked to the appearance of the Van Meter Visitor, but it could have created effects on a personal level for people in the town that we just aren't aware of.

The author (center) exploring Van Meter with fellow researchers Kevin Lee Nelson (left) and Chad Lewis (right)

The Mystery of the Plaster Cast

Another intriguing mystery involving the monster is the question of the plaster cast reportedly made by Peter Dunn after his run-in with the beast.

The morning after he blasted out the bank window and sash, Dunn had searched the area for signs of the creature. His singular find was a set of "great three-toed tracks." Dunn used plaster and made a cast of at least one of these mysterious tracks.

It's easy to imagine that the cast would have been of great interest to townspeople, especially those who had reported seeing the beast themselves. During the time period, such curiosities were usually put on display somewhere in town, frequently in a local business.

Dime Museums were also extremely popular during this time. Inspired by places such as P.T. Barnum's New York Museum, Dime Museums popped up all over the country and highlighted the odd, unusual, and downright bizarre. In an era when people were hungry for new entertainment, such places flourished. While there's no record of Van Meter having its own Dime Museum, it's possible that Dunn's cast could have been sold or sent to one of the regional museums.

It is, unfortunately, all speculation since there's no further record of the cast or what became of it. Chad Lewis pursued the mystery of the cast hoping to locate it somewhere in Van Meter, but the trail was long cold, and nothing ever surfaced.

Lewis points out that if the footprint had remained on display in a local business in the early 1900s, it may have been destroyed in the devasting fire of 1911, which decimated downtown Van Meter.

In their pursuit of the cast, Lewis, Nelson, and Voss also

learned that the cast may not have survived because of the material used. The authors report in *The Van Meter Visitor*:

"Several experts at the Iowa Historical Society stated that our search for the footprint may all be for naught, as they expressed doubt that a plaster cast from 1903 would have been able to survive such a long period of years. Their reasoning was that the plaster used in 1903 would most likely have been relatively soft and brittle, and unless it was properly stored (like in a museum), the odds of it not crumbling to pieces decades ago were very slim."

Personally, I like to hold out hope that somewhere in Iowa, there's an old box in someone's attic that holds a mysterious, still intact cast of a great, three-toed track. It would be a fantastic and significant find if such a thing ever surfaced.

The Mystery of the Plaster Cast

The Visitor Lingers

Although the events of 1903 are well in the past, there are some who suggest that the winged monster still lurks in the shadows of Van Meter. Some even claim they've seen it!

Chad Lewis has spoken frequently about the Van Meter Visitor. As one of the authors of an outstanding book about the monster, Lewis has received reports of strange flying anomalies in the Van Meter area that are similar to the winged creature reported in 1903.

Chad shared a few accounts with me from people who spotted strange creatures around the Van Meter area in recent years. These accounts were collected after the publication of Lewis, Nelson, and Voss's book on the Van Meter Visitor and as a result, none of them have been previously published.

The first report comes from a man who told Lewis that he'd grown up on a farm just outside of Winterset, about twenty-five minutes from Van Meter. The man recalled an event that took place on his family's farm in the 1960s when he was a boy. Although it was years later, he still remembered the event clearly. The man told Lewis that one night, his father rushed inside the house and said that "Dracula" was hanging on the side of a silo on the property. The witness's father grabbed his shotgun, rushed back outside, and fired at the beast. The man either missed completely, or, like the legendary Van Meter Visitor, the thing was impervious to bullets because it flew off into the night seemingly unaffected by the assault.

The father said that the creature was a bizarre-looking thing with "giant bat-like wings."

At one of the first Van Meter Visitor festivals, another man told Lewis that he'd spotted what looked like a giant bat just outside of town one evening in the 1980s. The man was out walking his dog along a gravel road near the abandoned coal mine when the incident occurred.

The witness told Lewis that it was just after dark when a bat-like creature with a four-to-five-foot wingspan flew overhead. The bat was the largest such creature the man had ever seen, and he grew concerned about his small dog. The man quickened his pace and headed for the safety of his home. The creature did not pass over again but the witness noted that when it first appeared, his dog had started whimpering.

He told Lewis that he never walked his dog in the area again after sighting the monstrosity.

During the 2017 Van Meter Festival, Lewis was approached by a man who said he'd seen a weird creature in the area in the early 2000s, shortly after he moved to Van Meter. The man was driving home around dusk one evening when he saw an unusual sight. Lewis told me:

"As he approached the area of the Veterans Cemetery (right outside of Van Meter) he saw what appeared to be a giant dead bat lying on the side of the road. Since he and his wife had their small children in the back seat, he did not want to stop to check it out. The next morning, in the safety of daylight, he went back to the spot and was disappointed to see that the creature was gone."

Accounts like those that Lewis has received raise interesting questions. It's unlikely that whatever is being spotted is the same creature that was seen over one hundred years ago, but perhaps these things are of the same species. So far, no modern accounts have surfaced that include the weird light or memory erasing odor, but maybe it's just a matter of time.

There's one final story to add. When I spoke at the Van Meter Festival in 2021, a woman named Sandra told me that she had seen a large, winged creature in the area in the summer of 2010. The woman and a friend spotted the thing near the old mine site. She recalled:

"We were driving around and we ended up on that dirt and gravel road. I learned later it's where the old mine had been. I pulled over as far as I could and then did a U-turn so we could head back to town. Just as I was coming out of the turn, my friend shouted: 'What's that thing?' It looked like a bat to me, but it was massive. With its wings open, it was way wider than my car. It was flying low and coming toward us from the field. I thought it was coming straight at the car and I sped up, driving way too fast down the gravel road. My friend was looking back, and she said it went up and over the trees on the other side of the road and then it was gone."

Were Sandra and her friend in the presence of Van Meter's strange visitor or one of its descendants? When I asked her what she believed the creature was, she responded: "I just don't know, but I know that it wasn't anything on record. It wasn't an animal that the world knows about."

Whatever still lurks around Van Meter, the town remains small and charming, and the specter of the strange events of 1903 still linger here and there. The town hosts an annual gathering, aptly named The Van Meter Visitor Festival, that acknowledges the monster and the weird events, drawing in those interested in the strange creature that once terrorized the small Iowa community. The festival grows each year and includes guest speakers, vendors, food, tours of the locations related to the monster, and maybe, just maybe, a chance to see something odd in the skies.

The Visitor Lingers

MONSTERS OF THE HAWKEYE STATE by David Weatherly

2

PART TWO
Bigfoot in Iowa

IOWA

Bigfoot in the Hawkeye State

Iowa is certainly not one of the top places one would expect to find Bigfoot. With its prairies, farmlands, and wide-open spaces, the automatic assumption is that there's nowhere for a large, bipedal creature to hide out and thrive. Some would even argue that Bigfoot could not possibly live in the state due to the lack of concealment the terrain offers. This, of course, is based on the common perception that the entire state is nothing but vast tracts of farmland and prairie.

Bigfoot researchers who have spent time exploring reports of the creature in Iowa note that many sightings in the state occur near the rivers where there's fresh water, food, and yes, places for the beast to hide. Interestingly, it's possible to travel a great distance through the Hawkeye State just by following the rivers. There are a number of parks and preserves in the state that also offer resources that a creature such as Bigfoot could take advantage of.

Beyond this, there's always the potential that the creatures aren't settled in Iowa but merely passing through on their way to the larger woodlands of neighboring states.

Historical Bigfoot data from pre-1940s is scant in Iowa, but, as we shall see, there are still some interesting encounters on record. Some reports are short on detail and leave us with only intriguing hints of something strange. For instance, rumors have long circulated that a population of monkeys live, or did live, in Preparation Canyon State Park outside of Moorhead in Monona County. As is par for the course, there's speculation that the monkeys had escaped from a circus in the 1930s.

Another legend involves the Ventura Marsh Monster, a large, hairy, shambling something that dwells outside the town of Ventura in Cerro Gordo County. Sightings are scant and often seem more like folklore or local legend but there's a possibility the tale came about because of early Bigfoot sightings in the area.

Ken Borrill of Clear Lake grew up in Ventura and recalled a local fisherman named Squire Davis who used to tell tales of the marsh monster. Davis called the creature a "mugwump" and said the thing came out at night. Borrill recalls the stories as typical, spooky campfire fare.

Wild Men

The earliest wild person account in Iowa that I've come across is not a wild man, but a wild woman. Legend says she was seen in 1884 around Gordon's Ferry in Jackson County. Cedar Rapids, IA's *Gazette* reported on the wild woman in its July 29, 1884, edition. According to the report:

"This queer specimen of female humanity was discovered by hunters in the woods. When first seen she was in an open space with her back toward them. Being anxious to get a good look at the strange apparition, the hunters endeavored to get in front of her, when, discovering them, she uttered an unearthly scream and darted off into the woods like a frightened deer."

The wild woman ran a short distance, then hid behind a tree, observing the hunting party with "a wild glare."

The men made another attempt to get a better look at the unusual figure, but she fled again, going deeper into the trees, and vanishing from sight. The men spent a couple of hours searching but could find no trace of her. According to the *Gazette*, the wild woman was described by the hunters as follows:

"They judged she was in the neighborhood of twenty years of age, with lithe and sinewy form, a receding forehead, and eyes which shone with an unnatural luster. Her hair they judged to be three feet long, and was black as coal, and hung in wild, disheveled locks near her shoulders. Her body was almost devoid of clothing, and her feet were bare."

There were various speculations as to the wild woman's identity, and one local put forth the idea that she was the missing daughter of an area farmer. Reportedly, the young woman was involved with a man, but her father refused to allow their marriage. She vanished and never returned. The speculation was that she had gone mad and perhaps turned to a feral existence in the woods.

A wild boy was reportedly spotted in East Davenport and Gilbert, both in Scott County, in the summer of 1869. According to the August 31 edition of the *New York Herald*, the boy was spotted by several individuals and was seen "prowling about the woods" on the property of a Judge Grant. According to reports, the boy, or whatever it was, stuck close to the river and was fond of fish. The *Herald* reports:

"About a week ago a man returning from a shooting excursion saw what he at first took for some wild animal crouching by the bank of the river. It suddenly plunged in and emerged with a fish, which it devoured ravenously. Getting closer to it, he saw that it was a boy, apparently about fifteen or sixteen, entirely without clothes, and covered with light, sandy hair of a silky appearance. He plainly saw the face and describes it as revoltingly ugly and brutal in its aspect. He attempted to approach it, but the creature became alarmed, and taking to the water, swam to a neighboring island and hid in the sedges. On returning home he gave information, and a close lookout has been kept. The creature, whatever it may be, has been seen twice since, and this wild boy of the woods will doubtless be shortly captured."

A wild man scare shook up Muscatine County in 1872. Laborers working on a division of the Muscatine Western Road reported the creature, describing it as a "wild man, gorilla, devil, or some like hideous apparition."

The May 30, 1872, edition of Muscatine's *Evening Journal* reported on the creature, stressing the difficulties the thing had caused for workers.

The thing was described as a "monster in human shape." Reportedly, it emerged from the woods and into a group of workers, terrifying them and driving them away in a panic. In at least one instance, the thing leapt out of a tree and attacked a man, tearing his clothing and running him off.

Col. Horton, who was in charge of the project, offered one teamster a carbine if he would return to work, but the man declined and said he wouldn't go back under any conditions. When pressed to relate what the beast was the man could only say that it "resembled a gorilla."

Another wild man was on the loose in the summer of 1883. According to the Janesville *Daily Gazette*, the creature had been lurking in the woods west of Iowa City in Johnson County. The paper's August 21 edition reported that the wild man had been seen by several witnesses. He was in a "semi-nude state" and had a "wild, uncivilized appearance." Locals tried to capture him but were unsuccessful in doing so.

Council Bluff's *Daily Nonpareil* reported that a "strange monster" was at large in the town of Diagonal in Ringgold County. The paper's September 28, 1899, edition said the thing had terrified some people a few miles from town.

No one knew whether the thing was a wild man or a wild animal that resembled a man. It was described by the paper as "of large stature, considerably more than six feet high, and covered from head to foot with long, black hair, either natural or the skin of beasts. Its color was very dark."

On September 27 the thing made an appearance at an area farm, the home of the Crook family. The beast entered the house through the back door making a growling noise as it entered. Mr. Crook was absent, but his wife, fifteen-year-old daughter, and an infant were at home.

The paper reported that the beast issued a "sort of suppressed roar and occasionally beat its breast. Mrs. Crook ran away from the house and fainted dead away just outside the door."

The fifteen-year-old showed more bravery. She grabbed the infant from its crib and prepared to defend the child, but the creature was occupying itself by rummaging through the family's pantry, throwing open doors in an apparent search for food. The young girl saw the thing's hunger and took action. As the paper reports:

"[She] placed on the table all the eatables available, which the wild brute instantly devoured, using both hands as a beast does its paws. When it had satisfied its hunger, it left the premises and walked toward the timber, distant about a half a mile from the house."

Just as the creature was entering the woods, a group of hunters arrived at the home. The Crook girl told the men what had happened, pointing out the wild man in the distance. The hunters immediately gave chase, but the thing had enough of a lead on them that it easily escaped.

The *Nonpareil* reports that the invasion at the Crook home wasn't the only appearance of the wild man; in fact, it seems the thing was quite active that day.

"About noon the children of Clayburn school saw the same object in the woods near the schoolhouse to which they ran for protection, barricading the door and windows, but it passed on without making any effort to enter.

"Later in the afternoon it visited the house of Mr. Frink, about eight miles north of Diagonal, and was seen by that gentleman, his daughter, a girl of 14, and a younger son. The two later were alone in the house at the time, but Mr. Frink drove up with a load of corn while it was standing in the door. As soon as the wild man saw him it gave a loud roar, and, jumping a fence without touching it, ran into a corn field."

Frink said he was certain the thing was an "immense ape or gorilla," and said the creature was covered in long, black hair.

The paper noted that a similar creature had been reported southeast of Afton in Union County. A hunting party was out looking for the creature but there's no record of anything more coming of the search.

What was assumed to be the same creature was also spotted in Madison County. According to Des Moines's *Daily Iowa Capital*, September 28, 1899, edition, the creature showed up around Macksburg.

A man looking for stray livestock in the Grand River timber was terrified when he came across the creature. The *Capital* reported that the wild man pursued the worker who ran to his horse and fled from the beast. The shaken man described the creature:

"The wild man was of gigantic stature, covered with hair, either natural or from some wild beast and looked like a gorilla or large ape."

The paper reported that other area residents, including a Mr. Prangle, and a Mr. Barman, had also seen the creature and put the community on alert. Reporters for the paper speculated about the creature's possible identity:

"If it is an insane man, he should be placed in an asylum where he cannot harm people nor frighten women and children; if it is a wild animal, it cannot be anything else but a gorilla, one of the most savage animals in existence and extremely dangerous when running at large."

Early Accounts

A mystery "ape-man" was terrorizing the city of Council Bluffs in Pottawattamie County in the spring of 1923.

A United Press story from March 20 said the creature had attacked fourteen people over a period of three weeks. The victims were women who reported that they were being attacked on city streets. One woman gave authorities a description of the culprit: "His arms are monkey-like, he slinks along in a stooped fashion, arms swinging loosely like those of a monkey."

The creature's attacks were like those of a wild animal. Reportedly the beast would sneak up behind women, snatch at their legs, and tear at their clothing.

Sheboygan, Wisconsin's *Press-Telegram* ran a story on the attacks, reporting that chief of police James C. Nicholl said that six women had already filed reports. He said getting victims to discuss the attacks was proving difficult as they were quite traumatized over the incidents.

Police officers were out in force hoping to find the attacker and the paper said they were using "football tactics" to effect the capture.

News reports emphasized that the attacker, whatever it was, was a cowardly sort and would flee if victims started to scream or fight back.

The March 21, 1923, edition of Cincinnati, Ohio's *Post* reported on the beast's attacks, recapping the known facts, and adding the tidbit that police officers disguised as women were patrolling the streets hoping to encounter the creature themselves.

The *Post* reported that the assailant was "a huge, ungainly creature, believed to be but half human, with most of the characteristics of a gorilla."

Additional information was provided by a victim who said the creature was "dark, heavy set, with a small, red face with long hair that covered his face, hairy arms and roughly dressed."

Most of the attacks happened around midnight and the attacker was prowling residential areas. It is curious that reports on the matter consistently stress the ape-like appearance of the attacker, so there are clearly unanswered questions on the matter.

Police chief Nicholl was reportedly investigating circuses who had winter quarters in the area and declared that he thought the thing "may be a monster monkey."

In the fall of 1930, a gorilla-like creature was reportedly seen on a farm near Glenwood, Mills County. A man working on the property was startled when the hairy creature approached a water tank, drank some water, then ran off.

The sighting was soon followed by another, this one in the town of East Emerson. The witness, Elmer Larson, was the night man at the Coggagae garage on Highway 34. At four a.m., Larson's attention was drawn to the sound of something soft footed walking on the driveway. Atlantic, Iowa's *News-Telegraph*, described the encounter in its October 6, 1930, edition:

"Elmer leaped out of his chair and had a mind to run, but his feet and legs refused to function, he said. There stood in front of the screen a monkey, nay, a hairy animal the size of a small man. The gorilla looked at Elmer for a time, and then cantered away and was lost in the darkness."

About a month later, the *News-Telegraph* reported on the hairy creature again, this time noting that it was "roaming the countryside surrounding the town of Atlantic in Cass County." The report added more background, stating that the beast had been present in the area for a year or more. The paper's November 6, 1930, edition reported:

"The hairy man-like monster has been seen a number of times during the last few days and is thought to be the same beast that has been roving over southwestern Iowa for the last year.

"Last fall a gorilla was seen by many farmers in west Pottawattamie County and several hunting parties were organized to kill the beast, which was terrorizing livestock on the farms, but no trace of the animal could be found by the posses."

According to the paper, the gorilla continued making the rounds and showing up at area farms. He was seen on the property of Sam Jensen and on the Fred Walter farm.

Mr. and Mrs Fred Scheef were husking corn one Saturday when Mrs. Scheef saw the creature in their cornfield. The paper reported that Mrs. Scheef watched as "the gorilla came down the corn row and watched her for several minutes, standing first on its hind legs and then flopping down on its forefeet, finally retreating without showing any viciousness."

Maybe it just wanted some fresh corn. Whatever the case, it stayed on the move, soon being spotted on another farm over a mile away, this one owned by Jim Wilkensen.

Fred Ruston and Charles Myers were on their way to the Wilkensen farm when they saw the creature. It was walking along a fence and when their car approached, it jumped over the fence and ran away in one of Wilkensen's fields.

Ruston and Myers hadn't heard the gorilla stories that were circulating and thought they had spotted a man in a fur coat. When they told Wilkensen about the weird incident, he told them about the ape thing being spotted in the area.

Blame was soon laid on a circus when Deputy Sheriff P.H. Edwards said he believed the creature was an animal that had escaped from a circus near Glenwood the previous year. Many doubted the explanation, pointing out that a tropical animal likely wouldn't survive the Iowa winter.

A farmer named C. Williams spotted the creature on November 17 and said that it was about the size of a man and the sighting helped launch a search for the beast at the Missouri River bottoms near Lake Manawa.

Large footprints were also discovered in the mud along the banks of Mosquito Lake.

As stories of the creature continued to circulate, the tales attracted more attention. A man named G.C. Bain showed up touting his expertise in tracking animals, based, according to him, on his experience with a Colorado sheepman's organization. The Associated Press reported on November 20 that Bain had proclaimed his skill at big-game hunting and set out on the trail of the gorilla.

Mason City's *Globe-Gazette* reported in its November 20 edition that Bain had examined the tracks found around Lake Manawa and declared them "unlike any he had seen before." He told reporters that he was putting baited traps out around the lake and expected to have the creature snared within a day or two. Of course, such plans rarely work out when it comes to monster hunting.

Mason City, Iowa's *Globe-Gazette* reported on the creature in its November 21, 1930, edition under the headline "Phantom is not 'Mere Monkey.'" The paper carried an Associated Press story, reporting:

"On the side of those who think Lake Manawa's phantom is more than a mere monkey today was aligned J. Miller, farmer, who has been added to the growing list of those who have seen the beast.

"While working in the field yesterday, Miller said, his horses started plunging wildly. 'I looked toward where the horses were grazing,' he said, 'and saw something ambling thru the corn rows. It was almost as tall as a man, shaggy and broad, but I couldn't say positively what it was."

Miller's farm was along the Missouri River where many thought the creature was lurking. Dogs in the area were also said to be very restless during the sightings.

Meanwhile, Bain, the Colorado trapper who was sure he would catch the beast, found it more elusive than he expected, and nothing showed up in his traps. He stated that he believed the creature was an escaped circus animal. Bain reportedly spoke with a hermit in the area who had heard the animal and reported that it issued an "uncanny wailing that put to shame the howl of a wolf and sounded like a woman being murdered."

While Bain continued his search for the beast, he was suddenly upstaged when another player entered the story—this one, a true showman.

The *Daily Nonpareil* out of Council Bluffs ran a story in its November 23 edition reporting that Colonel "Idaho Bill" Pearson of Hastings, Nebraska, had come forward claiming that the creature running around Iowa was none other than one of his escaped pets.

The *Nonpareil* stated that it had received a telegram from Chicago, Illinois, sent by the Colonel himself, announcing that he was preparing to travel to the area to retrieve the animal. The paper reported:

"In a telegram to the *Nonpareil* Saturday Colonel Pearson stated that the animal was in all probability one which escaped from his truck when it was turned over in an accident three weeks ago.

"While he did not classify the creature, the Colonel wired that it resembled a gorilla and was not dangerous and he begged hunters not to harm it."

Colonel Pearson was described as a "survivor of the old days on the plains. He still affects the goatee, long hair, and buckskin jacket of the old-time westerner."

In essence, Pearson was one of numerous wild west showmen who had modeled himself after the popular William Fredrick Cody, better known as Buffalo Bill.

The *Nonpareil* reported a bit about Pearson's reputation:

"It should be noted that Idaho Bill Pearson was a well-known showman who had no difficulty in spinning yarns. He supplied broncos to rodeos and is said to have roped and captured several bears. In a 1928 story, Pearson was traveling with a large feline, 'about twice as large as a mountain lion, with peculiar beard and markings similar to those of a tiger. Its ears resembled those of a gorilla. The colonel expects the animal, which he captured in southern Mexico, will be identified at the zoological gardens'"

It would seem that Pearson, having heard about the creature roaming the area, jumped into the fray to take advantage of the situation, either by generating publicity for himself, or by seizing the opportunity to claim possession of an unusual creature to utilize in his shows. Pearson of course had an answer that explained his connection to the beast. As reported in the paper:

"During his frequent visits to this city and to the home of his daughter in Shenandoah, IA, he had brought with him an animal in a specially constructed cage at the back of his truck and has offered rewards for any person who can name the beast."

Was it really Pearson's animal? It's doubtful and even the cover story doesn't make a lot of sense since there's no talk of previous displays of the creature in the area.

Whatever the case, Pearson got some publicity, and the hunt went on. People in the area remained worried for a time. Children were kept out of school or accompanied to and from the schoolhouses by their parents for safety.

Bain, the so-called big game tracker, and Colonel Idaho Bill Pearson both went along their way, and no one ever found the mysterious ape-like creature that had been roaming the country because it, too, went away and was not seen again. Perhaps it ran away and joined the circus.

A gorilla was purportedly on the loose in Wapello County in 1932. The August 24 edition of Carroll's *Daily Herald* reported that the beast was spotted near the city of Ottumwa by three men. They told law enforcement officers that they had seen the thing jumping up and down on a log.

In this case, the mystery was soon solved. People out hunting for the beast found a farmer named Andy Meyers, decked out in a horsehair coat with fur mittens on. Meyers wasn't attempting a hoax, rather, he was trying to get honey out of a beehive and had the gear on as protection against stings.

Residents of Webster County thought a chimpanzee was on the loose in the 1930s

People in Webster County said a chimpanzee was on the loose in their area in the summer of 1936.

The Connellsville, PA *Daily Courier* relayed the story out of Fort Dodge, Iowa, in its June 29 edition under the banner "Wandering Ape Hunted." According to the paper:

"Residents near Holiday Creek are searching for a mysterious chimpanzee which appeared in the vicinity late last fall. The animal survived the severe Iowa winter and has been seen lately searching for food. The chimpanzee is believed to have escaped from a circus cage."

A story from the International News Service on August 27, 1944, reported that a posse had been organized to hunt down a strange animal in Appanoose County.

A farmer named Bob Bear had spotted the creature on his property where it picked some corn which it placed neatly in a pile.

Those who saw the beast described it as "looking something like a monkey." It was reportedly brown to black in color with a grayish-white face. It was about the size of a large dog.

The creature was seen by a number of area residents, but the posse was unable to track it down.

Bigfoot researcher John Green reported having a news clipping (original source unknown) that mentioned Bigfoot sightings around the town of Maquoketa, Jackson County. Green notes that the article was published sometime in the 1970s, but the sightings went back much further.

The article mentions a woman living near the town of Baldwin who said that hunters and trappers in the area had long spoken of "animals that walked like men along the Maquoketa River near Canton. The woman had moved to the area fifty years previous and had heard the tales then. (This means she would have heard the tales in the 1920s.)

The article also covers an incident reported by twenty-one-year-old Maquoketa resident Gary Koontz. Koontz was out hunting in dense woods in the area when he saw the beast about a hundred feet from his position. He said it was standing upright on two legs, was between four and five feet tall, and covered with dark hair or fur. The face, he said, was flat. He also said the creature looked frightened. Perhaps it knew what was coming. Koontz stated:

"I knew it was something I had never seen before. I was

startled but decided to take a shot at it with my shotgun and I'm sure I hit it. It let out a high-pitched woman-like scream and disappeared into the brush" (Green, *Sasquatch the Apes Among Us*).

Koontz reported that his uncle, who was on leave from the army, had also seen a creature in the area around the same time.

The *Fairfield Ledger* included an interesting tidbit about an early Bigfoot sighting in its November 29, 1975, edition. Reporters with the paper spoke with Ramona Hibner who was associated with the South Mountain Bigfoot Research Group out of Brooksville, Florida. Hibner was looking into the Lockridge Monster sightings that were taking place at the time (covered later in this volume).

During the interview, Hibner stated that her father had seen a Bigfoot in the 1950s around Marble Rock. Marble Rock is located near the Shellrock River in Floyd County, southeast of Mason City.

A student at a Midwestern college in Dennison, Iowa, wrote to Roger Patterson in the late 1960s and reported that he and a friend had seen a Bigfoot in the woods behind their college one night. The man told Patterson that the creature looked like the one in Roger's famous Bigfoot footage (The Patterson/Gimlin film). John Green mentions the anecdote in *Sasquatch: the Apes Among Us*.

A BFRO report that deals with a November 1970 sighting has a note about an earlier account. The reporting witness, Jerry, writes:

"I also heard a scream in the late summer 1965 after dark behind my house here in grove of pine and apple trees. The dogs were barking, and this horrific scream started very loud and close. High pitched lasting at least 5 seconds, made my hair stand up, dogs stopped barking, probably hid. There were three more screams as it moved off to the east toward woods one mile away."

Jerry's '65 incident took place in an undisclosed location in Fayette County.

MONSTERS OF THE HAWKEYE STATE by David Weatherly

The Lockridge Monster

In the fall of 1975, the small town of Lockridge in Jefferson County was plagued by a mysterious beast that came to be known, fittingly, as the Lockridge Monster.

Most of the activity occurred in the Turkey Creek area, just north of Lockridge. The first notable sighting was on a Turkey Farm owned by Herbert Peiffer and his wife. The Peiffers had some kind of predator that had gone after their turkeys for several nights in a row. The beast was finally spotted on the evening of October 3, 1975.

That evening, Herb headed out just as the sun was going down to attend to his birds. He was driving his tractor out to the turkey pens when he spotted something in the vehicle's headlights. It was a dark colored, shaggy creature on four legs. Peiffer kept driving forward toward the beast, and he was shocked when the thing suddenly stood up on two legs and ran away from the area.

The Peiffers had been losing four to five turkeys each day. Almost every morning, they would find a pile of the dead birds on their property. Mrs. Peiffer pointed out that when predators such as coyotes killed turkeys, they would drag them off and the remains were rarely, if ever, found, so whatever was taking the birds in '75 was a mystery and the couple were truly puzzled. After Herb spotted the creature, speculation ran wild about what the thing was. Many people thought the farmer had spotted a bear. Mrs. Peiffer noted:

"Herb never did claim it was a bear, but what other animal is there that walks on all fours, then when it was startled by the tractor lights, stand up and walks forward on its hind feet?" (*Fairfield Ledger*, October 28, 1975).

Initially, Mr. Peiffer kept quiet about the creature on his

farm. He didn't speak out about his weird sighting until other area residents started to report the odd creature.

Around the same time, Mrs. Peiffer's father, E.W. Duttweiler, whose property was close to the Peiffers, found some unusual tracks on a sandbar along a nearby creek. The tracks couldn't be identified and, of course, this added to the mystery of the creature's identity.

Another area resident, Lowell Smith, spotted something in a field when he was driving to Mount Pleasant. Smith saw a creature in a cornfield that he first thought was a cow. He then realized that the four-legged thing, whatever it was, was black with long hair which is particularly un-cow-like in appearance.

Like Peiffer, Smith initially kept quiet about what he saw, but in true small-town fashion, he opened up when his mailman told him that one of his neighbors had spotted a weird animal skulking about.

It wasn't long before stories of the Lockridge Monster were making the rounds. Newspapers, radio, and television all started reporting about Iowa's latest monster.

The October 25, 1975, edition of the *Ottumwa Courier* contained comments from Lowell Smith's wife who tried to walk back her husband's report. She stated:

"Actually, my husband didn't see anything to talk about. He saw something but he wasn't close enough and didn't take the time to take a good look. He probably wouldn't have mentioned it if it hadn't been for the stories he heard about other people seeing something."

It seems likely that Mrs. Smith was trying to dismiss the entire incident involving her husband to keep her family out of the entire matter. Such a move is hardly surprising since many people in the community were, at this point, making fun of the whole monster tale.

The monster didn't care what people thought, though, and he continued to show up around the area.

Mrs. Gloria Olson spotted the beast when she was out one evening just before dark. Olson was driving past an old, deserted farmyard when she spotted something she knew was unusual. According to the October 27, 1975, edition of the *Muscatine Journal*, Olson reported:

"I slowed up and couldn't hardly believe my eyes. I didn't tarry too long. To me, it looked like it had a monkey's face, but I didn't study it too long."

Like many others, Olson had been reluctant to share her story. She told the paper: "When you tell people, they laugh at you."

She added, that if the creature was actually a person out for some fun, they were taking a big chance: "If they're playing a joke, they're sure liable to get shot."

An *Associated Press* story on October 29, 1975, reported on an area hunter named Lowell Adkins who found ten-inch tracks not far from the carcasses of four partially eaten turkeys. Some people thought the tracks were those of a bear that had made its way from Wisconsin or Michigan. Adkins himself didn't voice an opinion.

Even though other people had reported seeing the creature, almost all of the media focus was put on the Peiffers and it didn't take long before they were upset over the constant attention. The family was flooded with calls from reporters from around the country from New York to Texas people wanted to hear about the Peiffers encounter and their opinions on what the beast might be. In short order, the couple had monster fatigue. Mrs. Peiffer told reporters:

"'People keep asking me if it's a monster or something to do with devil-worship,' she said, 'and I keep telling them that we think it's a stray bear that's been killing our turkeys.'"

Texas's *San Antonio Express News* ran a story on the so-called monster hunt that was unfolding in the small Iowa town. The paper's November 9, 1975, edition announced: "Hunt for Mystery Monster," and reported: "A giant bear with the face of a monkey is being hunted in Lockridge, Iowa. The tracks are huge. A man with a size 12 foot doesn't even come near to filling them up."

The article mentioned the frustrations being experienced by the Peiffer family who were the focal point of the town's monster tale and Mrs. Peiffer said that local troublemakers were causing issues at the farm:

"Half-drunks in pick-up trucks are out every night looking for the thing and spooking the turkeys."

Peiffer also expressed her displeasure with the growing opinion that her husband was a fool, liar, or drunkard. "He doesn't even drink," she stated.

"If it's a bear, I hope that it stays around long enough to prove it so people stop thinking we're liars."

It wasn't long before a newspaper posed the question that was on many minds—was the creature a Bigfoot? The November 29, 1975, edition of the *Fairfield Ledger* presented the query in a headline:

"Lockridge Monster: Could It Be Bigfoot?"

The story reported that the South Mountain Research Group of Brooksville, Florida, was looking into the reports to determine whether the incidents matched other Bigfoot sightings. Ramona Hibner, a representative from the group, had contacted the Peiffers to get more information.

Into December newspapers were still running stories about the creature, even though sightings seemed to have filtered off. The Peiffers had shipped all of their turkeys off and, no doubt, they hoped it would be the end of the whole affair. A report in the December 15, 1975, edition of the *Des Moines Register* notes an odd thing that occurred on the Peiffer farm after the birds were gone, however. Mrs. Peiffer had discovered several partially eaten apples still hanging on the tree branches. The apples were about seven feet off the ground. "It looked like a bite was taken out of some of the choicest apples clear around the tree," Mrs. Peiffer noted.

Peiffer also told the paper that a hunter claimed to have seen the creature on their farm. The man had a camera with him but had no luck photographing the beast. "Before he got the camera focused, it was gone. He said he didn't know what it was, but it wasn't a bear," Peiffer said.

Tracks left behind by the creature showed five toes and were quite large. Peiffer noted that her son could easily put his size 12 shoe inside the prints. Some local hunters thought the prints bore a resemblance to bear tracks.

For a time, people continued to be concerned about the creature; it was, after all, an unknown and at the least it was killing farm animals. As a precaution, children were kept inside after dark, and people watched carefully for further signs of the beast.

Skeptics really didn't know what to make of the Lockridge Monster. The most common explanation offered was that it was a bear that had wandered into the area from parts unknown.

The explanation didn't sit well with many people. According to the Iowa Department of Natural Resources, the last officially recorded bear in the state was seen at Spirit Lake way back in 1876 and no one in Jefferson County had recalled ever seeing or hearing about a bear in the area.

Mrs. Peiffer, who seems to have wanted it to be a bear, was unhappy about comments made by state conservation officer Mike Sells, who said that he doubted a bear was present in Jefferson County. Peiffer said "He [Sells] has never contacted us to show him any tracks."

But if it wasn't a bear, what was the Lockridge Monster? One caller that Mrs. Peiffer spoke to represented a group in Pennsylvania. He insisted the creature was a pet that had been lost by aliens during a UFO landing.

Whatever the creature was, it moved on and left the small town of Lockridge alone, leaving in its wake a mystery that still puzzles people who remember the strange sightings.

Do monsters roam around the Iowa countryside?

The Lockridge Monster

MONSTERS OF THE HAWKEYE STATE by David Weatherly

The Ottosen Creature

In August 1978, the Humboldt County Sheriff's Office started receiving reports about an ape-like creature wandering around the small town of Ottosen.

Sheriff Marvin Anderson said the creature was described as hairy, about five feet tall and standing on two legs. The thing also reportedly had a "wide forehead."

Several locals, both adults and children, had reportedly seen the creature and some were concerned, noting that several pets in the area had been mangled to death during the time of the sightings.

Sheriff Anderson contacted neighboring county officials to find out if there was a missing ape or monkey on the loose. While he wasn't sure what the thing was, the sheriff thought there was a logical explanation to account for the sightings. Even though Anderson thought a known creature was to blame, he didn't rule out the possibility that pranksters could be at work.

The *Des Moines Register* reported on the creature in its August 2, 1978, edition, and said the first sighting of the creature had been the previous Monday when it was spotted heading into a cornfield just north of Ottosen.

On the afternoon of Monday, July 31, 1978, three boys spotted the creature. Steve Bennet, age 12, John Wolfe, age 11, and Greg Masters, age 10 were walking around near some livestock sale barns at the edge of town. One of the boys reported, "We were sort of goofing around and chased a cat up a tree. It was scared and it was bleeding." The boys weren't clear whether they were tormenting the cat or if they had just chased it, but either way, their antics were soon brought to an end.

The August 6, 1978, edition of the *Detroit Free Press* reported that the boys heard a "scratching noise" coming from one of the nearby buildings. In response, the boys threw a rock into the structure. When they did, a face appeared briefly in one of the windows. One of the boys described the figure:

"It was a big head, square-like. He had big eyes and a flat nose and broad shoulders. He was covered by black or dark brown hair."

At the sight of the thing, the boys fled the area. As they ran away, one of them looked back and saw the beast. It had dropped down on all fours and was running in "big leaps, its body hunched over as it vanished into a cornfield."

Later that evening, nine-year-old Donette Henkins stepped outside her grandmother's house and spotted the beast. The girl said that the creature had "deep-set eyes and fangs. It kind of growled and grunted," she said.

On July 30 Donnette's sister Dawn saw the ape thing. She was out on her bike that evening when she saw the creature about a block ahead of her. She reported:

"He just stood there. I couldn't see his face because it was in shadows. But I could see he was broad and was covered in hair."

Dawn screamed and several people sped to the area to see what was happening. Dawn's mother, twenty-four-year-old Pat Young, and twelve-year-old Gina Dahl all rushed to Dawn.

Stopping by the girl, the group heard a male voice ask, "Does anybody know what time it is?"

Mrs. Henkins's reported:

"I don't know where the voice came from, but we looked down toward the garage and saw this head looking at us around the corner. It had dazzling eyes; they were as big as golf balls. It had a big head covered with hair" (*Detroit Free Press*, August 6, 1978).

The women all quickly fled the scene. Henkins said she had no idea where the man's voice had come from, and that the incident was a complete mystery to her.

The Henkins family had good or bad luck, depending on your view, when it came to seeing the creature. Jan Henkins, who saw the thing on two occasions, stated, "It isn't anything like I've seen before; people think I'm crazy, but I know what I saw."

Henkins was so worried about the creature that she sent her two daughters to stay with her sister in Livermore. The girls had been very disturbed by the creature's presence. "My oldest daughter would wake up and just be shaking," Henkins stated.

Ottosen was, and still is, a very small town. At the time of the sightings, the population was just under 100 people. Today, it's even less—40 citizens according to the 2020 census. Given its size, one can only imagine the impact such a story had on the little community.

It wasn't long before word got out about the town's monster and people started showing up hoping to see it for themselves. Many of them were hoping to kill the monster.

Writing in the August 6, 1978, edition of the *Detroit Free Press*, reporter Frank Santiago painted a picture of what was happening in the normally quiet town:

"After the lights go out…the village of about 100 slips into a soft slumber in the middle of the cornfields that stretch to the horizon.

"But lately, Ottosen has been no peaceful, isolated respite. It has been more like Times Square. Trucks, cars, and motorcycles have roared into town, some of the occupants brandishing flashlights—and a few guns.

"The visitors have trampled through vacant houses and weedy lots, probing the shadows, and knocking on doors asking for directions.

"One resident, appalled by the intrusion, called Humboldt County Sheriff Marvin Anderson to complain that she couldn't safely cross the street in front of her home.

"The source of the commotion is stories of a creature lurking in Ottosen, a hairy, foul-smelling, 5-foot-high ape-like monster that growls and grunts and lives in the shadows."

Along with the sightings, there were other oddities that people believed were a result of the creature. On nights when the thing showed up, dogs in town would bark endlessly, sensing, perhaps, the monster's presence.

A woman named May Helieseth discovered that her grapevines had been stripped of both their fruit and leaves.

Of course, one of the most disturbing things was what was happening to people's pets. Residents' dogs, cats, and rabbits continued to disappear or turn up mutilated. Whatever the thing was, it was after more than just fruit.

Sheriff Anderson wasn't sure what he was dealing with. He told reporters:

"I wouldn't rule out the possibility of somebody wearing a costume. I would think he'd get by with it at night. But what has me puzzled is that one of the sightings was during the day. And anybody wearing a costume would be taking an awful chance. They could get shot." (*Detroit Free Press* August 6, 1978).

Officers from the sheriff's department started patrolling the town, both to help watch for the creature and to help manage the would-be monster hunters who flooded into town.

In mid-September 1978, a family living three miles northeast of the city of Humboldt in Humboldt County heard weird howls from something moving through a ravine near their home. The disturbing sounds started around midnight and were so disturbing that the family called the sheriff's office. Sheriff Anderson noted that the howls were so loud that he could hear them over the telephone. The following day, the sheriff went out to the property himself and investigated. He found areas where the brush was trampled but no tracks were visible.

Sheriff Anderson was also called on to examine an odd set of tracks discovered in an area cornfield. He found them odd, but he wasn't sure what had left them.

"I've never seen any like it before," he said. "There are three 'toes' on the front of the foot and one toward the back. We just don't know what it could be. It might be a bear, but then it might not. Some of the people said that it walks around on two legs and when it starts to run, it gets down on all fours. People are scared and mad. They don't want to go out at night and they're mad because people think they're crazy." (*Des Moines Register*, September 24, 1978).

Sometime around September 11, the creature showed up on the property of the Dodrill family, northwest of the town.

Anna Dodrill was standing at the kitchen sink washing dishes. Her normal routine took a turn when she looked up at the kitchen window and saw a face staring back at her from just outside. The *Des Moines Register*, September 24 edition, reported:

"Anna Dodrill froze with fear when she looked up from a load of dishes into the 'burning red eyes' of a big-nosed, black-faced, hairy-headed creature staring at her through a window a few feet away.

"It was the first time in my life I couldn't move."

The creature stared at the woman for a moment, then suddenly ran away into the darkness.

Earlier that evening, Anna's brother had seen a large, hairy arm reach out from behind a cattle shed when he was out on the property. The incident shook him up, and as a result, he was sitting in the house with a rifle at hand. He had not told any other family members about the arm.

Twenty-four hours later, September 12, the creature showed up about two miles southeast of Ottosen at the home of Robert Newell IV.

Newell heard a strange whining noise coming from his barnyard. Positive that it was not a sound from one of his farm animals, Newell looked out the window to see what was amiss. About thirty-five feet south of his house, he saw a tall, hairy hunchbacked figure go into his barn. Newell watched as the thing jumped into a manure spreader. After a moment, it climbed out and stood for a moment looking around. It then climbed into a grain spreader.

Newell thought the creature, whatever it was, was

searching for food. He continued to watch as it left the barn, walked around a grain silo, then quickly headed south into a recently harvested cornfield. According to the report in the September 24, 1978, edition of the *Des Moines Register*, Newell had a view of the black-haired beast for about three and a half minutes.

As September continued, officials in both Humboldt County and neighboring Kossuth County continued to receive reports of the hairy, bipedal creature. Still, no one was sure what it was. Sheriff Anderson told reporters:

"There really isn't much we can do. I believe these people saw something, but I don't know what."

Locals said the atmosphere in town had become very strange. Some took the matter very seriously while others joked about the whole thing.

Locals tried their best to deal with the unusual situation, and odd little incidents occurred as a result of the tension in town. One person walked into the local post office wearing a monkey mask. On an Iowa Highway 222 marker just outside of town, someone made an addition. Under the Ottosen town sign, they added another sign. This one read "Big Foot County."

Still, reports continued to come in about unsettling screams ringing out in the night. Cattle were being stampeded, and area pets continued to turn up dead. Kids were being kept in after dark, lest the monster show up.

"I tell you, if you're a nonbeliever, after you talk to a few of these people, you have to believe there's something there. I think those people have seen something, but I don't know if it's this Bigfoot connection they're talking about," said sheriff Anderson.

As expected, the topic was the constant talk of the town. Ottosen postmaster Edna Kampen said she heard about the monster on a daily basis. "At first, they thought it was a hoax, I think. But now there's been so many classes of people— farmers, townspeople, etc.—who saw it, that they're taking it more seriously." (*Des Moines Register*, September 24, 1978).

Mark Thompson, a farmer in Hardy, Humboldt County, saw a creature in his soybean field. He estimated that the thing was about seven feet tall. It was covered with brown-black hair.

Thompson drove closer to the creature, honked his horn, and flashed his truck's headlights at it. At this, the thing left the area.

The report about the incident in the October 1, 1978, edition of the *Des Moines Register* said that an "independent observer" visited the bean field and found prints in a nearby marshy area. The prints measured fourteen inches in length and were sunk two inches into the ground.

The October 1, 1978, edition of the *Des Moines Register* clearly had a tongue in cheek attitude when it ran the headline "Omah Gosh! Yeti Another Bigfoot Seen."

The paper reported that a group of forty high school students who had been working on a homecoming float on the night of September 27 spotted a pair of creatures in a nearby field. The students reported the odd detail that one of the creatures had red eyes and the other blue eyes.

"It had them scared," said sheriff Anderson, "it had them scared enough where they went to town and weren't going back out there."

The *Register* also reported that a fisherman in West Bend, Kossuth County, had discovered over twenty strange footprints under a bridge that spanned the west fork of the Des Moines River. Plaster casts were made of some of the tracks. They measured sixteen inches in length and five inches in width. Curiously, the tracks also had three distinct claws measuring three inches.

As the fall months unfolded, people around Ottosen were still on the lookout for the monster. The *West Bend Journal* reported on the creature in its November 9, 1978, edition. Interestingly, the paper implied that officials were seriously considering the potential of a Bigfoot with an article titled "Is Bigfoot Really Out There." The paper reported:

"Humboldt and Kossuth [County] sheriff departments,

who have done some research, believe that if Bigfoot exists, he may follow the Rock Island Railroad that parallels the west fork of the Des Moines River. So far, all reported sightings are only a few miles from this area."

Sightings of the Ottosen creature finally tapered off, or at least people stopped reporting it. Perhaps they were tired of the attention, or perhaps the thing shambled off to another place. Either way, the quiet town eventually returned to its normal everyday affairs and the mystery of the monster's identity was never solved.

The Ottosen Creature

MONSTERS OF THE HAWKEYE STATE by David Weatherly

Bigfoot Through the Decades

1970s

In the summer of 1970, a man spotted a large, brown colored creature in Clayton County about two miles north of the town of Monona. The creature ran across the road, down into a ditch, then leapt over a fence and ran off into a cornfield. There was a foul smell in the area, presumably from the Bigfoot.

The witness spoke to some locals who said the creature had been present in the area for a long time. The witness told the BFRO:

"Upon commenting about this to some elderly residents I was informed that the creature or creatures have been in the area for better than 100 years from old reports of them and intermittent cattle and sheep mutilations."

The area is comprised of rolling hills, a cornfield and a large, wooded area. The location is a few miles from the Yellow River bottom.

A group of college students traveling through Fayette County in late November 1970 spotted a Bigfoot as it crossed the road during a snowstorm.

The group of four was driving on a country road near the town of Maynard. Their progress was slow—they were going about twenty miles per hour—due to heavy snow. The reporting witness was in the back seat, leaning in to watch the road ahead when something big started moving from a field up ahead. The witness shouted and the driver slowed down further. The group observed the creature as it stepped over a forty-inch-high fence, moved through the ditch, and crossed the road where it stepped over another forty-inch-high fence.

The group was only fifty feet from the thing and had a good view of it as it moved past their vehicle. Jerry, the reporting witness, described the creature to the BFRO:

"It was big, at least 8 feet tall, covered from coned head to feet with dark brown hair. It had a barrel-shaped body with long arms and legs. It just walked like a human taking long strides and swinging its arms. It crossed at an angle from NW to SE, never turning to look at us, so we did not see its face."

Stone Park, site of a strange Bigfoot encounter in the 1970s

One of the creepiest encounters from the 1970s occurred in the summer of 1971. Gary Parker and two friends were driving into Stone Park, a state park and wildlife sanctuary a few miles from Sioux City in Woodbury and Plymouth Counties.

On their way in, a vehicle full of terrified teenagers rushed past them. Parker and his companions didn't know what to think but continued into the park to have a look around. They followed the road to the upper region of the park where they parked and exited the vehicle. They soon noticed that a strange silence hung over the area. No birds or other wildlife could be seen or heard, not even insects.

The three men did spot a living creature though—something standing at the top of a hill. The creature was outlined by the evening sky. It was large, dark, and ape or manlike in form.

Initially, the men were more intrigued than frightened. They were all in their early twenties and in strong physical form. What happened next, however, was not what they expected. Jerome Clark detailed the incident in the Summer 1975 edition of *UFO Report*. He writes:

"Suddenly, for no discernable reason, one of the group, George Fetterman, let out a Tarzan cry and beat his chest, which immediately attracted the creature's attention.

"Suddenly the thing started toward them. It disappeared from sight into the trees but by the sound it made, there was no question of its direction or purpose. In the frantic moments that followed, the men noticed that the creature's feet made a dragging sound, as if the animal were injured. But still it was moving fast and as it advanced, a stream of animals—squirrels, foxes, rabbits, birds—blind with terror, poured out of the woods."

Like the animals, the three men went into a panic. They jumped into the vehicle and raced out of the area. They were in such a hurry that the car hit a fox, but the animal survived. It jumped back to its feet and continued running from the scene along with the rest of the retreating animals.

As the group was leaving the area, Gary Parker looked back. He saw the tall, dark form come out of the trees in the area where they had been standing moments before. They had escaped just in time.

A couple of days later, Parker talked to a gas station employee close to the park. The man said that a group of terrified teenagers had stopped at the station the same night that Parker and his friends had their encounter. The attendant said the teens had asked for a rag to wipe something off their vehicle. Clarke reports:

"The grill was covered with blood. They explained that they had been driving near the park when suddenly a "man" loomed in front of them. Before the startled driver could hit the brakes, the car collided with the creature, which then reeled over, got to its feet, and ran off. Stunned—they knew the impact should have been hard enough to kill a man—the teenagers realized that, whatever they had hit, it was not human. They left the area as fast as they could."

The teens were almost certainly the same group that Parker and his friends had seen racing away from the park when they were entering and apparently, they were responsible for the injured Bigfoot that came after the Parker group.

An article in the March 9, 1980, edition of the *Des Moines Register* detailed a 1973 encounter from Delaware County. According to the story, Delaware County Sheriff Bert Elledge spoke to a witness who saw a frightening creature just north of Manchester. According to the paper:

"That sighting, in September 1973, was reported by Jerry Ewing, who at the time was a service manager for a Manchester auto dealer. Ewing, who now makes his home in Colorado, said in a phone interview last week that on the day of the sighting he had driven his pickup truck into the country. 'I intended to spend my noon lunch period hunting squirrels.' Said Ewing. 'I drove about five miles north of town and pulled into a clearing. I got out of the pickup and in a field about a hundred yards away I saw a strange man-like animal walking alone. It was about a foot taller than a normal man and was covered with hair and it was big, real big, going at about 400 pounds. I'm a hunter and I've seen lots of wild animals but I've never seen anything like that before. I couldn't believe my eyes.'

"'It went into some woods, then came out and looked at me. We looked at each other for maybe five minutes. I wanted to get a better look but all I had was a .22 (.22-caliber rifle) and I didn't want to get too close.'"

At around one thirty a.m. on January 1, 1974, Sioux City resident Jim Britton had just bid goodnight to some friends in the driveway of his home. While he was outside, he had noticed a shadowy figure moving behind some cars. Although he noticed the movement, he dismissed it, thinking it was likely a neighborhood dog.

Once he was back in his home, Britton was startled to hear a high, shrill scream. The sound was like nothing he had heard before. Looking out the window, Britton saw a large, gorilla-like figure outside his home. He quickly grabbed his 30-30 rifle and rushed outside. The creature he saw stood upright like a man and was about seven feet tall. It was hairy and its forelimbs hung down to its knees. The thing started to approach him and when it was around 75 feet away, Britton let loose with his gun. The creature fell backwards, but quickly sprang back up on its feet and ran from the scene on all fours at a high rate of speed (Green, *Sasquatch: the Apes Among Us*).

In the time it took the man to reload his rifle, the creature had vanished. An inspection of the area the next day revealed no prints but some traces of blood indicating that Britton had hit the creature.

A family traveling through Scott County in April 1974 saw a Bigfoot standing in the middle of the highway.

The reporting witness who recalled the event filed a report with the Oregonbigfoot website. The witness was about eleven years old at the time and was in the backseat of the vehicle.

The incident occurred near the Martin Marietta Cement Plant outside the town of Buffalo. It was a dark and moonlit night with clear conditions.

A woman was driving, and her adult daughter (the reporting witness's mother) was in the front passenger seat. The woman alerted her mother that there was a "cow loose on the road" ahead of the car.

The two women began to discuss the odd appearance of the figure, running through various possibilities to explain what it was. The driver slowed down and the witness's mother stated, "It looks like a man in a thick, dark coat."

The driver suddenly commanded everyone to lock their doors. She sped up and swerved to miss the figure that was on the highway. The witness recalls that the thing was in the middle of the road picking something up off the highway. The online report states:

"My mom told me years later that it looked like a very tall man with a black, furry wool coat, bending over at the waist and very intently picking up something in the middle of the road.

"As they passed, she noticed that it was about 3 ½ or 4 feet tall. And if it stood up it would have been 7-8 feet tall, approximately 400-500 lbs.

"She had been an RN and was good at guessing others' weight within a few pounds."

The *Des Moines Register* (December 12, 1978) noted a curious but unconfirmed incident:

"There is even one unsubstantiated report from a Sioux City research group that a man wounded a Bigfoot with a deer rifle in 1974 near Stone Park on the northwest edge of Sioux City."

My friend and colleague Linda Godfrey received a report from a man who said he had encountered a "Bigfoot-like" creature in the late summer of 1974. The incident occurred about six miles northeast of the town of Mediapolis in Des Moines County.

The witness, Jack, was riding a motorcycle and was on his way home. Godfrey shared Jack's report in her book, *I Know What I Saw*. The man wrote:

"On my way home, I was going down a dirt road close to [my house]. The road is flat, then becomes hilly. As I crossed a creek and came up over the first hill, I saw something dark, huge, and unbelievably fast. It ran down a fifteen-foot embankment across the dirt road and jumped the fence in what seemed like five strides."

Jack reports that he quickly hit the brakes, left his motorcycle, and pursued the creature on foot. He told Godfrey the thing was moving through the trees "like a bull elephant."

The man chased the creature for about forty yards, then suddenly stopped, his instincts telling him that he better leave the thing alone. Though he was bold at first, the witness suddenly became terrified and ran back out of the forest as quickly as he could, reaching his motorcycle and racing for home.

Jack told Godfrey that he has never been so terrified of anything before or since. That day marked the last time he had entered that area of woods and in the aftermath, anytime he was near forested land in the area, he carried a firearm with him for protection.

Strange things were afoot in the Riverside area of Sioux City in August 1974. Events began when citizens called authorities to complain about a weird howling sound that was disturbing residents of a housing development along the city's Riverside Boulevard.

Some people pointed the finger at one local man, assuming that the noise was being made by his watchdog.

When a police officer was dispatched to check on things, he spoke with the resident and verified that it wasn't the man's dog at all. The sound, the man said, was coming from behind his home from the vicinity of two partially completed houses.

The police officer could hear the sound clearly and he was so disturbed by it that he retrieved a shotgun from his patrol car before investigating further. Along with the man he had spoken to, the officer searched the area around the partially constructed homes. A half an hour of investigation led to the discovery of a small, black puppy that the officer decided was the source of the weird noise. The civilian was doubtful that the puppy could be making the weird sounds.

Returning home, the man found that his watchdog had been so worked up by the noise that it had broken its chain trying to escape.

Residents of the quiet area were about to have more than just weird night howls to deal with. As Jerome Clark writes in the summer, 1975 edition of *UFO Report*:

"Another resident who lived in Riverside...saw a very hairy, ape-like creature squatting in her backyard garden eating tomatoes. The thing, which appeared to be about three and a half feet tall, was approximately 100 feet away. The woman grabbed her children and called the police, who found primatelike footprints on the ground in and around the garden."

During the last week of August, another resident, "D.S.", also spotted the creature. The man woke to the sound of his back porch rail rattling. Getting up to investigate, he looked out to see a man-like creature shuffling by. The witness estimated the creature weighed around two hundred pounds. He said it was very hairy and one of its arms drooped about six inches lower than the other.

The man watched as the thing walked across his lawn. He told police officers: "It didn't run from the yard but merely walked away, dragging its feet." (Clark, *UFO Report*, Summer 1975).

Police officers Steven Bernard and Glenn Groves of the city's K-9 division arrived at the scene to investigate. Along with their dogs, they tracked the creature to an eight-foot-high chain link fence surrounding the property of the Riverside Junior High School. The tracks ended at a locked gate and despite a thorough search of the area, the police officers could find no further trace of the creature. It was as if it had just vanished.

The *Sioux City Journal* reported on the bizarre beast in its August 31, 1974, edition. The publication of the story prompted another area resident to come forward, though she asked to remain anonymous. The woman reported that early on the morning of August 30, she had been roused by her dogs barking frantically and the sound of her front gate rattling. "My dogs are too small to rattle the gate," she reported, "and the neighbor's dogs have never rattled it before."

The woman got up to see what was causing the commotion. Since it was still dark out, she grabbed a flashlight and directed the beam down from her second story window. The light startled a figure which jumped down from a ten-foot-high stairway and ran into her garden. The creature was out of her view, but she could hear it making a strange sound, one she described as "a gurgling sound which started deep in the throat and then just came out in a loud screech. It was a piercing sound. You would never forget it." (*UFO Report*, Summer 1975).

Other people living in the area also reported that their dogs had been very disturbed on the same weekend. Jerome Clark's article mentions another interesting tidbit about Iowa creature sightings:

"According to Bob Brienzo, a graduate student in English literature who is intimately familiar with the manimal reports of the area, several farmers near Hinton, Iowa...have complained for years that some kind of biped—which they have not seen but whose tracks they have spotted many times—has been disturbing their cattle and sheep."

At 7:30 a.m., on August 10, 1976, Melvin E. Dreier was headed to one of his farm properties to feed cattle when he spotted some strange tracks on the gravel road. Examining the tracks, Dreier discovered that they went for about half a mile.

Dreier, a resident of Dumont in Butler County, later contacted Bigfoot researcher Grover Krantz about the track find. Dreier took photos of the tracks which he sent to Krantz.

The prints measured 12 to 13 inches long and were 5 inches wide. Stride length was about six feet. Dreier compared the impressions with his own size ten shoe print. His two hundred and thirty pounds barely showed in the gravel and dirt road. The tracks had come from an area of open country and headed toward a wooded area that paralleled the West Fork River.

A report in the August 26, 1976, edition of the *Sibley Tribune* says that a thirteen-year-old boy named Dan Radunz saw a six-foot, black hairy creature near the Ocheyedan River around 9:30 on the morning of August 22. The creature was holding its hands together, giving the impression that it was drinking water.

The boy was riding in a car with his family when he spotted the thing. The vehicle was crossing a narrow bridge spanning the river and the boy had a clear view of the creature. Lest one think the incident was the young man's imagination, there was more to the story.

He hadn't told his parents about the sighting, and to his credit, he was questioning the sighting. He told the paper:

"I was so surprised I thought my imagination was playing

tricks. I had watched a television movie the night before called "Mysterious Creatures." One part was about the Bigfoot creature in the Pacific Northwest. Now, right on the banks of a river near my home, here was a Bigfoot! I had to be seeing things."

Later in the day, the boy's parents asked young Dan what had disturbed him so much. He told them about what he had seen, and, the next morning, they all went back to the location of the boy's sighting. Searching the area, they discovered fourteen-inch footprints that were narrow in the heel but seven inches across the five toes. The prints extended from a woodlot down to the water and back again. There were no further signs of the creature that had left the tracks.

The *Tribune* report also included comments from Iowa Bigfoot researcher Cliff LaBrecque who said he'd seen Bigfoot himself—"fifteen or sixteen times." LaBrecque said all of his sightings had occurred in southern Iowa.

LaBrecque was an active Bigfoot researcher at the time and had commissioned a full-sized replica of the famous hairy creature.

The *Tribune* reported that the replica was built by Deaton Museum Studio, a company known for natural history exhibits. The model was made of reinforced fiberglass and was covered with nylon hair. It took six months to complete the almost one-hundred-pound figure. The paper reported:

"The finished product is surprisingly realistic. LaBrecque purchased a trailer so the model could be transported for display at the Iowa State Fair, and at shopping centers in Iowa, Michigan, Oklahoma, and Florida. He does not charge admission to view his monster but does solicit purchases of T-shirts and posters decorated with monster prints. The profits help defray traveling expenses and further searches."

LaBrecque and another Bigfoot investigator, Kevin Cook, were the founders of "Bigfoot Research, Inc., of Iowa." They both reportedly quit their jobs in order to pursue Bigfoot full time.

LaBrecque says he was attacked by a Bigfoot in 1977.

According to his account, he had been monitoring a group of Bigfoot in area on the outskirts of Des Moines for a period of two and a half months. He says things took a turn when he decided to shoot one of the creatures. His encounter, listed on the *Bigfootencounters* website, reads in part:

"It was about 25 feet away from where I parked in my pickup truck. Two of the creatures walked up from behind a hedge. One stopped but the other went to a woodpile, bent down, and started to eat with [its] back towards me. I stayed in the car and waited for it to turn around, but it just kept gnawing at the wood. Finally, I decided to shoot it from behind. When the animal turned and saw me, I got buck fever and couldn't shoot. As it came towards me, I couldn't get the window rolled up fast enough."

LaBrecque claims that the eight-foot-tall creature then reached in through the window, grabbed him, and shook him viciously, so much so that he passed out. When he regained consciousness, the creatures were all gone.

The model that LaBrecque commissioned was in part based on the creature that he said attacked him. Details were obtained during hypnosis sessions LaBrecque had done in order to remember the event more clearly.

In 2014, LaBrecque put his Bigfoot model up for sale on Internet auction site eBay—starting bid--$85,000. There were no takers.

A brief note in Ray Crowe's *Bigfoot Behavior Volume II* reports an unusual sighting from 1977. A witness watched a "small Bigfoot" picking up frogs along the Shell Rock River. The creature would eat the head and body of the frogs, then discard the legs. The thing also left ten-inch tracks behind.

Another report from 1977 claims that an Iowa man tried to shoot a Bigfoot. Purportedly, the man had "lured a group of the creatures to his backyard on a number of occasions by leaving food out for them." (*East Jackson County Examiner*, July 31, 1999).

The man claimed that the creatures varied in size from eight feet down to four feet. The Examiner reports that one night the man decided to shoot one of the creatures, but before he could fire, one of them grabbed him. The man blacked out and the Bigfoot dropped him. It left the area but not before smashing the windshield of the man's car. The events were reported by a witness who claimed to have watched the events unfold.

A report in the December 20, 1977, edition of the *Oskaloosa Herald* notes that a woman named Therese McGee saw a creature near a coal mine near town. The beast was between eight and ten feet in height and had "bristly-like fur." The witness had gone out to sweep away some snow when the thing jumped out from the shadow of a tree with its arms out.

Rife's *Bigfoot Across America* notes a 1978 incident from Dallas County (date not given). Reportedly, several people spotted a Bigfoot around the Raccoon River. In one instance, a man was walking to his cabin and startled a black-haired Bigfoot that was napping. The creature quickly got to its feet and ran from the area. The witness said the thing was about seven feet tall.

Around the same time, a farmer in the area saw a pair of creatures walking along the road near one of his fields. One Bigfoot was around seven feet tall and the other slightly shorter, around six feet. Both were covered from head to toe with black hair. They had long arms and short necks. The man saw them from a distance of about one hundred yards.

On January 1, 1978, a woman living near the Skunk River northeast of Oskaloosa, Mahaska County, reported seen a Bigfoot step out of the shadow of a tree during a heavy snowstorm. She said the creature was between 600 and 700 pounds and stood eight to ten feet tall. A few days after her sighting, another area resident heard unusual noises around his home and discovered strange tracks in his yard (Des Moines Register, December 12, 1978).

February 25, 1978, a young boy said he saw a Bigfoot on the road near the Old Pella Bridge in Pella, Marion County. The boy said the creature stopped and looked at him briefly, then vanished into the surrounding woods.

Matt Ver Steeg, an investigator with the Iowa Bigfoot Information Center, went to the scene to investigate. He followed the creature's trackway into the woods but by the time he arrived the tracks had filled with snow making further determinations impossible.

Ver Steeg did note that the young boy was so shaken by the incident that he refused to leave the house for several days.

Throughout 1978, the Iowa Bigfoot Information Center received numerous reports of sightings and anomalous sounds from an area around Stephens State Forest. The area is certainly prime territory for a creature such as Bigfoot to call home. The woodland area is Iowa's largest state forest and totals over 15,500 acres stretched across five counties.

On August 28, 1978, a pair of high school students in Moulton, Appanoose County, saw a creature on a dirt road in an area known as Sedan Bottoms. The pair spotted the beast around 10:30 at night. They said it was between seven and eight feet tall and weighed around 400 pounds.

The following day, they took their science teacher out to the scene, and he discovered a three toed footprint measuring fourteen inches in length. The group also discovered trampled brush and some corn that had been stripped down to the cob (Des Moines Register December 12, 1978).

In early October 1978, a woman in Clarion, Wright County, contacted authorities to report a dark image that was peering through her kitchen window around 10:30 at night. The window, on the backside of the house, was a full seven feet off the ground, so whatever was looking in was quite tall. Some evidence at the scene suggested that this incident may have been a hoax.

A woman listed as "Babs W." was pulling into the drive of her home and saw a Bigfoot walking across a field and into the Backbone State Park in Delaware County. The incident was related to the BFRO by a man named Jerry who had his own Bigfoot sighting in November 1970 (detailed earlier in this chapter).

The incident from Babs occurred in late fall 1979. The report notes that the woman had reported hearing unusual screams and howls that went on for several days and frightened her horses. She reported the incidents to a park ranger who told her she had probably seen a bear. The woman was confident that what she spotted was not a bear. It walked on two legs, and as she watched it, it stepped over a high fence.

The road into Backbone State Park

The October 28, 1979, edition of the *Des Moines Register* reported on an incident from Webster City in Hamilton County. Forty-eight-year-old Bryon Davis was out looking for raccoon tracks in a wooded area near the Boone River when he came across a large creature sleeping on the ground.

Davis told reporters that the creature was about 450 pounds and had long, thick red hair down its shoulders. Davis's presence disturbed the creature which rose quickly and left the area in fast "five-foot strides."

The witness also said that the Bigfoot stood straight on two legs like a man but didn't look like a human or ape. He said that he was within eighteen feet of the thing as it strode into the woods.

Davis said he wasn't scared but dumbfounded. "If he had

been walking towards me, you bet I would have been scared," the man added.

Davis contacted authorities and reported the sighting. He also volunteered to take a lie detector test to prove he was telling the truth. "There's no joke about this," he said. "I supposed a lot of people don't believe...and are laughing. I could care less."

Bigfoot was wandering around Dallas County in November 1979, leading to an investigation by local authorities.

Larry Wilson of rural Minburn, called the sheriff's office to report a strange sighting at his property in the vicinity of the Raccoon River. Wilson reached deputy Craig Hein who was on duty that night. Wilson said he was alerted by the barking of his dogs around nine o'clock and stepped outside his sliding glass doors to look around. He heard a heavy, rhythmic breathing but couldn't see the source of the sound. To get a better view, Wilson went upstairs and looked out of a window onto the yard. He spotted a creature, illuminated by a security light about forty yards from his house. The November 16, 1979, edition of the *Des Moines Register* reported on the incident:

"Wilson described the creature to Hein as a 'hunched over, dark thing.' Hein said Wilson would 'not commit himself to saying it was hairy,' but he said it looked just like the pictures and drawings he has seen of Bigfoot."

Hein and another officer went to Wilson's house and discovered trampled prints in the frost covered grass. The prints measured 13 inches in length and the creature's stride was measured at forty-eight inches from toe to toe.

The creature was only under the security light for a couple of seconds, so the witness didn't get a look at its face. According to the paper, Wilson stated:

"It looked like a man in a gorilla suit. I really couldn't estimate its height. It walked with a fairly long pace, and it had a definite arm swing. It might have had stooped shoulders."

Wilson added that he had always been a skeptic about Bigfoot, but the sighting had frightened him and given him a different perspective.

"I have hunted, fished and been out in the woods a lot, but I never saw or heard anything like that before. It was unnatural."

The Dallas County Sheriff's office planned to have deputies search the area more thoroughly to look for evidence of a human prankster. Officials were concerned that if the sighting was the result of a human out trying to pull a hoax, the suit wearing miscreant might get shot by a jumpy local.

Local papers were hot on the story for a few days but there was little to follow up on beyond repeating Wilson's report. Deputies searching the area found nothing to indicate that a hoaxster was at work and the large footprints remained a mystery.

Could Bigfoot survive the harsh Iowa winters?

1980s

On January 15, 1980, railroad engineer Cyril O'Brien saw a strange creature near the tracks around Manchester in Delaware County. O'Brien said the thing was bent over and appeared to be feeding on the corpse of a cow. O'Brien told T.J. Ryder, reporter with the *Des Moines Register*, that the creature was "the meanest looking animal" he'd ever laid his eyes on.

According to an article in the *Register's* February 6, 1980, edition, O'Brien, 62, had been traveling the rails for thirty-eight years and had never seen such a beast. He told the paper:

"It was big, much bigger than a dog, and at first, I thought it might be a calf. It was a heck of a mean-looking thing with long, yellowish hair, a flat face, and short ears. It had no tail."

As O'Brien's train approached, the creature looked up and moved backwards away from the area. The engineer reported that the beast moved on all fours. When he spotted the thing, O'Brien radioed back to three other trainmen who were in the caboose. They too spotted the creature and like O'Brien, had no idea what it was.

O'Brien's sighting was one of several that occurred in the area in the early months of the year. On January 23, two men were out on their land north of Manchester looking for sites to plant some trees when they came across some unusual tracks in the snow. The prints measured 9 ½ inches in length and 4 ½ inches in width. The creature was bipedal, and the tracks showed that it had six toes.

The men contacted Delaware County Sheriff Bert Elledge who investigated the scene and took photographs of the tracks. Elledge, a long-time hunter, had never seen such tracks and showed the photos to state conservation officer Jim Becker for a second opinion. Becker was unable to identify the creature that left the prints.

In its Sunday, March 9, 1980, edition, the *Des Moines Register* reported on Bigfoot again with the headline "Bigfoot Rears His Hairy Head in Iowa Again."

The article, once again by T.J. Ryder, noted that Delaware

County Sheriff Bert Elledge had received numerous accounts of some kind of strange creature wandering the county. "There's been too many sightings, these people have got to be seeing something," Elledge stated.

The sheriff had taken the reports seriously enough that he had begun carrying a tranquilizer gun with him. The paper said that since the O'Brien sighting on January 15, the accounts had grown significantly:

"Delaware residents—solid, practical men like the sheriff himself—have come to Elledge with tales of a strange-looking creature roaming the countryside. On his desk, the sheriff has a file that has grown thick with the testimony of what they've seen."

The sheriff related an incident that occurred just prior to O'Brien's sighting. According to Elledge, on January 13, two men from Edgewood came to see the sheriff about a weird creature they had encountered. The men asked the sheriff to keep their names confidential but the February 24, 1980, edition of Waterloo's *Courier* published the account revealing one of the men was named Tim BuShaw.

The pair were driving south out of Edgewood, eleven miles north of Manchester, when they spotted a large, bipedal creature step onto the road. The creature had come from an abandoned farm property in the area and initially it moved toward the vehicle for a few steps, but then turned away. The creature was illuminated by the vehicle's headlights. The *Register* provided further details of the sighting:

"It was about seven feet tall and weighed about 350 to 400 pounds. They said it had a large chest and very long arms and moved in an upright position.

"They also said it had a topknot on its head (a sort of pointed crown of hair or bone) and that long hair extended from the topknot to its shoulders."

The men returned to the scene during daylight hours hoping to track the creature, but they were unable to do so.

A pair of men out hunting in Warren County in the fall of

1982 saw a Bigfoot while they were sitting in a hunting blind. It was November 13, around ten a.m., and the two men were watching for geese near a soybean field, about a mile outside the town of Carlisle. They spotted movement toward the east and observed a creature between seven and eight feet in height, walking in a bent over position. The witness told the BFRO that the creature "walked faster than we had ever seen a human walk."

The creature was black, and hair covered, and the men observed it from about 100 yards away. After the thing had left the area, the hunters went to look for tracks, but the ground was frozen, and no prints were visible.

The BFRO received a report from a woman who spotted a Bigfoot on July 15, 1983, in Greene County. It was around midnight and the witness was sitting on her back porch waiting for her boyfriend to stop by after he left work. From her position, she had a view of the road and she watched anxiously for the headlights of his truck. Due to the time, there was little to no traffic on the road, and as she watched, she saw a figure step out onto the road about 150 feet from her position. She recounts the incident:

"It crossed the road very near the streetlight, which illuminated it very clearly. It stood approximately 7 feet tall, had medium to dark brown hair covering its entire body, and was walking upright. It was very broad through the chest, and I was near enough to be able to see the muscle outline of its right arm."

The witness says the creature was "in no hurry" and that it vanished behind the shrubbery that lined a neighbor's driveway.

The neighbor had hunting dogs that he kept penned in the back yard of his home, and moments after the witness lost sight of the creature, the dogs started barking ferociously.

Behind the witness's house was a cornfield, and not far away was a stream with fresh water and a wooded area, a seemingly prime area for the creature to find food and water.

In the BFRO's follow-up report, it's noted that people in

the area had reported livestock damage, something that was blamed on local dogs.

Reportedly, a truck driver traveling through Estherville, Emmet County, in 1989 saw a large, bipedal creature cross the road in front of his truck. The man said the thing was about six feet tall and had brownish orange hair.

This report was sent to me by an associate who did not have further details or the original source.

1990s

An artifact hunter out searching in Decatur County had a startling encounter with a massive Bigfoot in September 1991.

The witness told the BFRO that he was in a public area north of Highway 29 one afternoon and intended to hunt in a creek that he had not visited for some time. He encountered two men in the area who said they were hunting. The witness felt uneasy about the pair and went to a point further from their location for safety. In short order, however, the men had moved and were close to his position. Feeling uneasy about the situation, the witness decided to abandon his hunt and go home. He climbed out of the creek to head back to his truck. He was not at all prepared for what happened next.

The man was suddenly in front of a massive creature that was sitting on the ground with its back leaning against a tree. The witness reports that the beast would have been twelve feet tall if it were standing up. The man reported:

"I was only 20 ft. from this thing…It was sleeping with its hands and fingers locked together stretched out across its knees. There were massive amounts of leaves in its very long brownish hair which covered it head to toe, including the face."

The man felt "nauseous and confused" when confronted with the sight and he jumped back into the creek to get away from it. At that point, the creature rose and took off in an easterly direction.

The witness says that he has not returned to the creek since his sighting, and he has heard of various hunters and fishermen who have spotted something similar in the same area.

A report on the Oregon Bigfoot website comes from a man who said he and his wife spotted a Bigfoot in Woodbury County in 1993.

The man was driving near the town of Climbing Hill one evening and his wife and young daughter were with him. A few blocks after crossing over a bridge, the witness's wife shouted out as something approached the vehicle. The man recalls:

"This thing walked up to the car and looked right at us. My wife screamed. Right then it turned and walked west about two blocks, turned south into the corn that was ten feet tall. This thing was almost that tall! The fur was red. It had the biggest arms and shoulders I have ever seen."

The reporting witness notes that there had been bad floods that year and that area rivers were all overflowing their banks.

Iowa resident Roger Price reported a series of Bigfoot related events that took place between 1992 and 1996. He doesn't provide the locations of the incidents, but says they began in August 1992 when he was pulling his boat in one evening around 8:20. A terrible stench filled the air, a smell like rotten eggs or sewage. Around nine o'clock, a figure was spotted that resembled a bear walking on its hind legs. One of the men present fired three quick shots with a .22 rifle and as a result, the creature moved quicky and vanished. Price gave investigator Tim Olson information about the sightings and Olson related the details he received in the March 1997 edition of *The Sasquatch Report*. The issue included a description of the beast provided by Price:

"The creature appeared to be 6' 5" to 6' 10" tall, with a thick square-type body. Its arms were big and heavy, reaching just past the kneecaps. It had what appeared to be thick, mossy, brown hair with inverted eyes which were close together. When it walked, its arms swung way in front and way in back. Approximate weight of the creature is estimated at 275-325 lbs."

Price also told Olson about another encounter from the

summer of 1995. The incident occurred on July 18 at 1:30 a.m. Price and a companion were in a wooded area and heard a "loud, sharp, whistling" sound. Ten to fifteen seconds later, they heard "an ungodly sound...like that of a screaming woman."

The men turned on spotlights and saw a creature walking nearby. The thing was initially walking toward the men, but after the lights were shone on it, it entered a shallow river and vanished. Price states, "We think it may have gone under the water and swum below the surface and exited some point where our lights were not shining."

This creature was reportedly larger than the previous one Price described, coming in at an estimated 350-400 pounds and standing about seven feet tall.

Price also experienced other incidents during the period. The rotten egg smell was frequent, and the odd whistling sound was heard on other occasions as well. Price reported finding prints that measured 13.5 inches in length and 6.25 inches in width.

Iowa's *Sioux City Journal* ran an article in its August 9, 1997, edition headlined "Bigfoot and Family Visit North Side."

The article, by Jennifer Palmer, reported on some incidents taking place on the north side of Sioux City in Woodbury County. Local resident Lori Gabriel told the paper that while she hadn't seen the creature herself, she had frequently heard strange noises around her house, usually between midnight and five a.m. She also reported finding footprints in her backyard. As she told the *Journal*:

"The last four or five nights we have heard branches breaking, and there have been footprints everywhere. Now I found three different sets of footprints. It looked like Bigfoot, his mate, and baby Bigfoot might have made them, like they were standing next to each other."

Another area resident, James Corbin, did spot the beast. He called the Sioux City Police Department to report the incident. According to the *Journal*, Corbin said the thing was "taller than 7 feet with reddish-brown hair." The witness described his sighting to reporters:

"I woke up about 5 a.m. and saw this huge thing outside my window. It had its back to me, and I did not get a good glimpse of it because I did not have my glasses on at the time. I had to squint to see it well, then it just disappeared."

Lori Gabriel also reported that footprints had shown up in the yards of other area residents. She said that someone, or something, had been letting her dog off its leash at night. She found it puzzling and reported, "My dog doesn't let nobody touch him unless one of us is out there."

Many strange sightings occur along Iowa's rivers

Bigfoot researcher Bobbie Short received a report about a July 1999 incident that occurred in Dallas County between West Des Moines and Van Meter.

The witness and some friends were out camping in the timber to celebrate the beginning of their summer vacation. (The group were high school students.)

After some time talking around a campfire, the four companions turned in and bedded down in a tent. Sometime later that night they were awoken by odd sounds outside the tent. The reporting witness says the noise was "a strange grunting sound, sounding like some sort of sick cow or something, and heavy, raspy breathing."

The group also noticed a foul stench like that of rotten eggs. The four considered that perhaps a raccoon or other animal was after their food, but the sounds were unlike anything they were familiar with.

They exited the tent to investigate, and when they did, the sounds suddenly stopped. At that point, they caught sight of the source of the disturbance—a creature close to seven feet in height with reddish brown fur.

Apparently startled by the campers, the creature took off. The witness described the thing to Short:

"His body was pretty strange as to the proportion question. Big hands (most likely big feet too), tall, and large biceps and upper leg muscles from what I could tell, and long hair covered his whole body from what we could see."

A witness told the BFRO about strange incidents in Jasper County that included foul smells and a blood curdling growling/howling sound. The witness also spotted a strange figure, red/black in color in August 1999. No detailed description of the creature was provided but when spotted, it was moving on all fours. The witness notes that the location is close to the South Skunk River and wildlife is plentiful in the area.

A man named Todd Davis told the BFRO that he and a friend were camping in Wilson Island State Park on December 12, 1999, when they heard some disturbing sounds. The park is in Pottawattamie County and abuts the Desoto Bend National Wildlife Refuge.

Around eight o'clock in the evening, the men heard a couple of screams that sounded like a woman crying, or the sound of an animal being killed. Aside from the disturbing sounds, the wooded park was very quiet and still and the pair believed they were the only ones out camping in the area.

They soon turned in, but their night was not a peaceful

one. It was almost three a.m. when Todd was awakened by the sound of heavy footsteps in the dry leaves around his tent. He listened quietly as whatever it was circled around the tent and stopped just behind his head.

Initially, Todd thought his friend Brian had gotten up to use the bathroom, but then he heard his friend climbing out of his own tent and he became alarmed.

When Todd rushed out to join Brian, the creature that had been stalking about their camp fled the area, rushing into the darkness and toward the Missouri River.

"Neither one of us saw anything but I have never felt like that before. The whole night we both felt like we were being watched."

Todd told a BFRO investigator that he had listened to online recordings of purported Bigfoot vocalizations, and they matched what he and his friend had heard that night.

2000s

A thirty-year employee of the Iowa State Department of Revenue, Jim J., saw a creature in Polk County in February 2000. Jim was close to the Des Moines River on a bike trail between Birdland Marina on its south end and Big Creek on the north end. Jim was making his way down the trail when he spotted a deer coming in the opposite direction. The animal kept looking over its shoulder and seemed nervous. The witness soon saw the source of the deer's attention—a large, dark creature. Jim told the BFRO:

"At first, I thought it was a human being. I mean, it had a head, shoulders, arms and legs, chest. It saw me at a distance of about three hundred feet and when it saw me it kind of hunkered down."

Jim, who has a degree in anthropology, said that after the creature crouched down, it suddenly sprang into action, turning 90 degrees, leaping into the air, and fleeing the scene rapidly. He says the beast moved two to three times quicker than an Olympic class sprinter could run and it was soon out of sight. He described the creature as about six feet in height, black and slim.

A man out hunting in Marion County saw a white Bigfoot on October 24, 2000. The man was close to the town of Pella, in a public access hunting area. He had his four-year-old son with him, and the pair were observing a crane that had just taken to the sky. Forty yards away, the man saw a bipedal creature run across the trail ahead of him. He said the creature was extremely fast and quiet as it moved.

The man and his son sat down and loaded his gun before going over to the spot where the creature had passed by. The ground was covered with leaves and no prints were visible.

The witness told Bigfoot researcher Matt Moneymaker that the creature was "a tall, upright-walking man-shaped animal covered with white fur."

It's notable that the location of the sighting is only a mile or two from the Des Moines River. Moneymaker notes that a large portion of Iowa Bigfoot sightings occur within a few miles of the river.

A couple driving in Buchanan County on July 16, 2004, saw a massive Bigfoot near the Wapsipinicon River.

It was 6:30 in the morning and the couple were driving on a country road on their way to a relative's cabin. They noticed a foul odor fill the air and soon after the stench hit, they spotted an "ape-type thing" in the road about fifty yards ahead. The Bigfoot was about seven feet tall and covered in reddish-brown hair. It had an ape/human-like face and its head sunk into its shoulders with little neck visible. The creature's hands went down below its knees and the thing's estimated weight was around 500 pounds.

The creature paused a moment, then walked off with long strides and was quickly out of sight. The woman thought the creature's eyes were red in color. Both witnesses were reluctant to talk about the incident and the woman found it especially upsetting.

The Wapsipinicon River

A report on the *Bigfoot Encounters* website details a sighting by a fisherman outside the town of Follets in Clinton County.

The incident took place on October 22, 2006. The man and two companions were out fishing on the Wapsipinicon River hoping to catch some catfish. They arrived just before sunset, built a fire, and put their lines in the water. The temperature was around 35 degrees, and as darkness fell, the men stayed by the fire.

The witness says he had fished the river on other occasions and was used to the normal night sounds of small animals coming to the river to forage. On this occasion, however, he heard what sounded like a larger creature on the other side of the river about 100 feet away. The man stepped away from the fire and let his vision adjust to the darkness. Scanning the area, he spotted the source of the sounds he had heard—a large figure, about seven feet in height and well over three hundred pounds. From its movements, the witness believed the creature was foraging for food.

The man went back to the fire and told his companions about what he had seen. He retrieved a flashlight, and the three men went back over to the river away from the fire. The reporting witness turned his flashlight on the creature. Caught in the beam of light, a large, hairy creature was visible. When the light hit the beast, it fled quickly into the woods and was gone.

The man continued to search with his flashlight, hoping to see the thing again, but it never reappeared. The men stayed in the area until around two a.m., but there were no further incidents.

A man out hunting in November 2006 saw a creature in Washington County. The man was on his way back to his truck when a noise drew his attention. Thinking it was perhaps a deer, the man drew his gun and sighted in with his scope. He saw a large creature moving at incredible speed.

In a conversation with the BFRO's Steve Moon, the man said the creature was only 30 to 40 yards from his position when he saw it. It was around 5:30 in the evening and visibility was good.

The man told Moon that as the creature fled, it held its arms up at shoulder level and "made boxing-like movements as it ran."

The creature was very tall and muscular, and covered with hair. Since the thing was running away, the witness was unable to see its face.

The shaken hunter "took off in a dead sprint back to his truck," and left the scene. He returned with a companion the following day and looked around the area. He reports that the area the creature was running through was near a dry riverbed and was comprised of dense brush and trees.

According to a BFRO report, a man out hunting in Lee County had a terrifying encounter in mid-April 2007.

The man said that he was on private property near the Shimeck State Forest Croton Unit. He was in full camouflage and had gone out early in the morning to take up a position and wait for turkey. He set up on a hill overlooking a small creek and valley. It was pitch black when he took up his position, and it had been raining, but soon the sky cleared, and the woods became bright.

The man soon realized he was within fifteen feet of several turkeys that were roosted in a tree. He had his gun propped on his knee and had put a decoy out close by. He watched the birds as the sky continued to clear but his attention was drawn to an unusual noise in the distance. He says the sound had a "strange pace," and he could not identify it. The sound grew louder, and the man realized that whatever the source was, it was moving through the valley, coming toward his position. The turkeys also heard the noise and they fell silent. Suddenly, the birds dropped to the ground and raced away from the area as if they were startled and greatly alarmed by something.

Unsure what had spooked the birds, the man continued to sit silently and watch the area as the sound came closer and closer. He soon saw the source of the sound, and it was like nothing he had ever seen before. "To this day, I will never forget what I saw in the coming moments," he reports.

"At first, I thought it was a hunter in a ghillie suit. But upon closer examination I realized this was no human wearing a camo outfit."

The creature was over six feet in height and very broad shouldered. It had long arms and was covered in either hair or fur that was dark gray in color. The witness said the creature appeared filthy and had a bad odor.

When the witness first saw the creature, it was about 50 yards from his position. It walked upright on two legs and as the man watched, the creature stopped. The hunter adds: "When it stopped and stood still it became nearly invisible in the forest."

The man realized what he was seeing, and he was greatly disturbed by the sight, but things were about to get even more unsettling. He reports:

"What happened next scared me so bad I would have bet my life that I was going to have a heart attack. The creature turned its head and looked directly at me. I stared directly into the eyes of this creature for an unknown amount of time. It made no sound, it did not move, only stared at me. I was in full camouflage including a facemask so maybe it was not sure what I was."

The hunter began to shake uncontrollably and the only thing he could think of was defending himself. He clicked the safety off his shotgun and the sound caused the creature to suddenly go into a crouching position, as if it were getting ready to move quickly.

The hunter and the creature continued to stare at each other. The man adjusted his position, moving his hands on the shotgun. At the movement, the creature also sprang into action, quickly moving into the trees and away from the scene. As it did so, it continued to watch the hunter until it was out of sight.

"I jumped up as soon as it was gone, and I ran back to my truck without stopping to rest once. To this day I will never forget what I saw or the feeling of absolute terror that overcame me."

The man says that he has not, and never will, return to the area of his encounter.

A man driving through Madison County in the fall of 2007 spotted a Bigfoot on Hogback Bridge Road.

It was mid-November about 11:30 at night and the witness was on his way home after visiting his parents outside of Earlham. His wife and daughter were with him in the vehicle, but both were asleep.

When the man approached an intersection in the road, he saw something crouched by the directional sign. As he got closer, the thing stood up and the driver thought it was going to try to cross the road. He told the BFRO:

"My heart skipped several beats at the sheer size of this thing. It was easily 7-8 feet tall, was very skinny/lanky, and was covered with shaggy, matted brown hair. Its eyes reflected yellow in my headlights like a cat's.

The frightened man swerved his car and kept driving away from the creature.

The area is mostly pastures and farmland, but a small creek runs parallel to the road on the side that the Bigfoot was standing.

The Sasquatch Chronicles Blog has a report involving a Bigfoot at a military base in the fall of 2008.

The reporting witness asked to remain anonymous and said that the incident occurred near the end of October. He states that he was working on a 19,000-acre, secure property that had armed guards on patrol.

It was around six o'clock in the evening and the man was driving a truck over some rough country on his way to help some other workers. As he drove, a figure on a ridge line caught his attention. He stopped his truck and backed up to get a better view of the object. He reports:

"This thing appeared to be 7 ½ foot tall or better. Probably around 5-6 hundred pounds. Dark hair...just looked like a huge gorilla, walking on 2 feet—only with longer hair. When I say hair, I mean all over its body. There was no neck, and it had a cone head."

The witness said the creature was about a hundred yards away and he had it in view for about three minutes. The Bigfoot never looked in the man's direction. It walked down a draw and was soon out of view.

The man reports that the base is still an active military installation and people are not allowed to freely roam the property.

The March 2, 2009, edition of Burlington, Iowa's *The Hawk Eye* ran a headline that proclaimed, "Bigfoot Sightings Reported to Iowa Conservation Office."

The article noted that the creature had been reported in Jefferson County but that Shawn Morrissey, operations and natural resources manager for Jefferson County Conservation, thought the sightings were a case of mistaken identity. Morrissey told the paper that he had received several reports, one from the summer of 2007, another in the fall of 2008, and another in the spring of 2009. Regarding the witnesses, Morrissey said:

"It's my own personal feeling they saw something that tricked their eyes and was a very explainable animal."

Morrissey went on to tell reporters that people who had reported Bigfoot had likely seen a hunter in a ghillie suit, or a horse.

Like me, you may find yourself reading that last sentence twice and shaking your head at the absurdity that anyone would mistake a large, common, four-legged animal for a Bigfoot!

Nevertheless, Morrissey seemed confident that there was not a Bigfoot anywhere in Iowa, adding "It's unlikely a large, fur-covered biped could play hide and seek in Iowa wilderness and remain undocumented. The state simply doesn't have enough large stretches of timber where such a creature could live."

In August 2009, a man out for a walk in the countryside had a Bigfoot sighting near Vinton, Benton County.

The man had walked for a couple of miles and the sun was setting, so he decided to head back home. On his way back, he noticed a neighbor's dog was barking at something in the road. The witness didn't see anything, so he continued his trek.

A few moments later, a foul odor filled the air. The witness reports that the stench smelled like a combination of wet dog, skunk, and rotten eggs. The man was nearing a trailer on the right-hand side of the street and the odor was getting stronger and stronger.

A lamp post beside the trailer cast a dim light on the man's path, and he stopped at this point to change the music on his audio player. While doing so, his peripheral vision caught movement in a nearby ditch. At first, he thought the movement was from wind hitting a tree, but the "tree" suddenly stood up. The account on the *Your True Tales* website reports:

"He snapped his head to the right and what he saw he will never forget. It had to have been at least ten feet tall and covered in reddish brown hair. It had an oval head that connected directly to very broad shoulders. It was facing away from him, so he didn't see its face."

The man watched as the creature, moving on two legs, walked up out of the ditch and into a field. It entered a tree line and right after it did so, the night rang out with a blood curdling scream.

The terrified witness ran home.

At a grocery market the following day, the man overheard some of his neighbors talking about the disappearance of two young calves the previous night. Branches on trees near the cattle had been snapped off and saplings ripped out of the ground, adding to the man's disturbed feeling about his encounter.

A father and son night fishing trip took a turn in the fall of 2012 when several creatures showed up at the witness's fishing spot.

The man and his son were out in Dubuque County on September 21 and were behind the Sundown Mountain Ski Resort. The pair were in a public access area off of Twin Springs Drive. Although the area is public, it is somewhat secluded and wooded.

Sometime between 7:50 and 8:30 p.m., the pair arrived at the water's edge and sat down on a couple of buckets by the creek. After they started fishing, they began to hear sounds in the woods nearby. At first, the witness assumed some raccoons were active since they are common in the area.

As the sounds continued, the man noticed a large figure on the other side of the creek. In the moonlight, the witness could tell that it was a large, bipedal animal. It moved to the top of a rock outcropping across from the father and son and stood between two trees. The figure then squatted down and sat watching the fishermen.

The man reports that he was intrigued, though his son was scared by the situation. Things would quickly become concerning, however. As the witness reported to the BFRO:

"Within 10 minutes another came to join the first to his right and stayed just across a ravine. No more than 6 minutes later another came from the south, just to the left of the one squatting across from us. As this one got close, it let out a piercing shriek.

Nothing like the calls that are heard on the TV shows. This was high pitched and frightening."

The fishermen quickly grabbed their gear and fled to their vehicle.

A 2012 report listed on the BFRO website details a truck driver's sighting of a very large Bigfoot in Boone County.

It was November when the witness was traveling eastbound on US 30, descending into the Des Moines River Valley. It was around twilight when the man saw three deer burst out of the trees and run across the road ahead of his semi. The driver, a seasoned hunter, said the deer were in a full run with their ears back. He soon learned why. He told the BFRO:

"I started slowing down and maybe 75 yards behind them a very large, bipedal object was running behind them."

The witness estimated the creature was between eight and nine feet in height. It had matted hair "a little darker than a chocolate lab." The creature's hair was of varied length, and the face was bare with visible skin that was two shades lighter than the thing's hair.

The large creature crossed the road quickly, moving from the center ditch on the side and across the eastbound lane in a mere five or six strides.

The sighting occurred near the Des Moines River.

Another BFRO report gives details of a July 2012 sighting in Dallas County near the town of Perry.

The witness reports that several members of his family were camping on their property west of the Raccoon River near a heavily forested area. There was a campfire going and there were numerous noises coming from the surrounding woods, including the sound of branches breaking, knocks and "thumps."

The sounds continued for about an hour and the reporting witness finally got up to investigate. He walked about ten yards from the fire and peered into the area where the sounds had been heard.

"All of a sudden, something about waist high ran very fast in front of me. To this day I don't know what it was; I turned and about nine feet away I saw an eight-foot creature staring at me. I did not get any facial details. I was too far away from the fire. I could tell that its head had a point on top."

The creature's eyes glowed red, and the thing stared at the boy for about ten seconds before it turned and disappeared into the darkness.

Six months after the incident, the young man and his parents were out fishing on their property when they found a fifteen-inch footprint near a pond.

Two years later, the young man and his father were camping in the same area and discovered another footprint—this one measured twenty inches.

A large creature was spotted crossing a road in Hardin County in the spring of 2015.

It was almost midnight on May 14, and the witness was on his way home from work. The man was driving up a hill when something leapt onto the road at the top of the hill.

He told the BFRO that the thing was black, had red eyes, and was extremely large. It moved quickly and vanished into the woods on the opposite side of the road from which it had emerged.

Bigfoot researcher Steve Moon followed up on the report and notes that the area is rich in resources:

"The area where this encounter occurred is a dense greenbelt along the upper reaches of the Iowa River. The Iowa is quite small here, but is mighty, having carved a deep canyon through the heart of what is now the town of Iowa Falls, which is just a few miles upstream from the encounter. There are numerous wildlife management areas, county parks, and boat access parks for many miles along this stretch of the river. This greenbelt is quite extensive, with bedrock outcrops along the river."

The June 2, 2018, edition of the *Okaloosa News* out of Okaloosa, Iowa, reported on a Bigfoot encounter from

Mahaska County. Under the headline "Tall Hairy Creature Startles Fisherman," the paper detailed an incident from Lake Hawthorne.

According to police officer Kevin Lamberson, who took the report, a man living in the city limits of New Sharon saw a six-and-a-half-foot tall creature that was very large and very hairy. According to the official report, the witness stated that the creature was "covered in black and brown hair, and you couldn't even see a face it was so hairy."

The sighting occurred between eight and eight thirty in the evening and there was still light for visibility. The witness told Lamberson that he spotted the creature on the opposite side of the lake and that it entered the water and swam towards his position. The paper reports that the creature "swam across the lake and proceeded to follow him as he left in his truck. He was unsure what the thing was, a person or an animal."

Officer Lamberson alerted both the Mahaska County Sheriff's Office and the Iowa Department of Natural Resources about the incident.

The December 18, 2020, edition of the University of Iowa's independent newspaper, *The Daily Iowan*, reported on the search for Bigfoot in the state.

The paper spoke with brothers Seth and Jesse Alne, who had a strange encounter in 2009 in the Waterloo area.

"The Alne brothers split down a trail to avoid trekking through a flooded area when Jesse saw a large hairy creature approaching. It was huge, with red eyes that were glowing in the night. The creature pushed over a massive tree and glared at him with intent."

The creature ran away into the woods and Jesse shouted out to his brother that he had seen a Bigfoot. The bold pair began to chase the creature as it barreled away. It quickly outpaced the Alne brothers and vanished.

The brothers say they're still unsure exactly what they saw, but the experience inspired them to search for further evidence of strange things lurking in Iowa's woods. They initially formed a paranormal group since they were also interested in ghost hunting, but eventually put focus on the search for Bigfoot after hearing about more accounts in the state. Seth Alne told the paper that the night he and his brother had gotten lost in the woods was a turning point for them:

"It led to a pretty insane run-in, especially for Jesse—it was his first sighting. And it all just kind of pushed us over the edge. And that was back in 2009 that we really started diving after Bigfoot."

A comment on the *Daily Iowan's* webpage on the story comes from a sixty-six-year-old retired woman named Linda McQuerry. McQuerry reports that she was snowed in at her cabin on eighty-six heavily timbered acres in rural Davis County.

"In late January I experienced 5-6 nights of stench, whistles, and frightening howls outside the cabin. I never saw anything, but I saw 4 huge footprints that were 5-toed and very wide, lacking the arch. I heard many strange sounds coming from the woods and heard many sounds of trees and limbs and falling crashes in the days and weeks leading up to this time."

McQuerry also reports that wildlife is abundant in the area, and that she's very familiar with the locally known creatures. Whatever was lurking around her cabin was something very different. "There's something there, definitely," she adds.

Another commentor on the story, JJ Hoffman, reports that he his father's property abuts a Wildlife Management Area, and that he had put IR (infra-red) trail cams out to see what he could catch on video. Hoffman reports:

"I have several videos with something very large and dark just out of range of the light. It will stand there and look at the camera with red eyes and you can see its shape moving around but not what it is. I can't find prints, but I know it's not deer. I don't hunt there even after I have permission, it's too damn spooky."

Several news sources picked up on a Bigfoot sighting reported by a man out walking in Dubuque County in the summer of 2021.

Jake Truemper, a radio host with K92.3, shared the news on his blog on July 22.

The witness, listed only as Jeremy, was out for a morning walk with his sister in Whitewater Canyon in Bernard. He told Truemper that he had spotted an unusual figure:

"I pointed out the figure and my sister laughed, saying it was a person. We called out to it but got no response. You don't have to believe me. I wouldn't believe me, but now that I've seen whatever that was firsthand...I think I may be a Bigfoot believer now."

The witness took a photograph of the figure, and the images were circulated online. While there have been other reports of Bigfoot in the area, most cryptozoologists were not impressed by the photo.

Does a population of Bigfoot live in the Hawkeye State? The jury is still out, but at the least, the history of encounters indicates that the creatures travel through at times and take advantage of the state's resources.

As more and more people join the search for proof of the existence of Bigfoot, Iowa may prove a surprising source of evidence.

MONSTERS OF THE HAWKEYE STATE by David Weatherly

Bigfoot Through the Decades

PART THREE
Weird Things in the Hawkeye State

Curious Beasts

A journey through early Iowa newspapers reveals brief entries here and there of strange animals reported in the state over the years. Many of the entries are short and scant on detail but interesting, nonetheless.

A snippet from the August 9, 1887, edition of Dubuque's *Daily Herald* mentions an oddity spotted in Dubuque County. The creature was described as a "nondescript animal, a mixture of monkey and baboon, caught on the bluffs in the rear of the brewery, a curiosity of the four-footed tribe."

The April 21, 1892, edition of the *Brownstown Banner* reported on an "Iowa Freak" noting: "A Marion County physician is the owner of a remarkable human monstrosity, a male child, 16 inches long, weighing 9 ½ pounds, its head the perfect counterpart of that of some gigantic serpent."

No doubt, P.T. Barnum would have been happy to snag the thing for his museum. Another oddity is mentioned in a brief note in the July 31, 1913, edition of the *Hardin County Ledger*. According to the news item, a "mysterious animal" had been spotted again. "This time by the boy Lloyd, who was at the barn just after dark. He said it was white and as large as a sheep."

The vague description leaves nothing to go on and the animal could have been anything. Apparently, it had been seen previously and the fact that it was white in color may have led to its classification as something mysterious.

Mason City's *Globe-Gazette* announced the capture of a strange animal in its November 4, 1929, edition. According to the paper, the beast appeared to be a cross between a coyote and a police dog, but displayed a "greater ferocity than either."

It was caught in Clear Lake in Cerro Gordo County.

A man named Ed Teake caught the animal at the Windsot Silver Fox Farm. The paper reports that the creature had been causing problems around the farm for a time:

"It had been noticed prowling about the farm where it had been stalking and eating pheasants. After being confined to a pen at the fox farm, it attempted to escape by gnawing the bars and woodwork. It greatly resented the approach of persons to the cage, growling and snapping when anyone drew near."

Another strange animal showed up in the fall of 1945 in Washington County. According to the September 29 edition of the *Washington Evening Journal*:

"C. G. Anderson, living five miles southeast of town, said today the strange animal that has been seen and heard in the county in the past several weeks, was at his place early Wednesday, killing one chicken. It was just as described by others whose farms it had visited, leaving a strange track in the mud and being unusually quick in its movements."

We could easily presume that the chicken thief was something common like a fox, but the news bit indicates there was a strange quality to the beast.

Washington is part of Iowa City's metropolitan area and even in the 1940s there would have been plenty of people living in the area so it's curious that there are not more reports about the animal.

Unusual Swine

The November 8, 1907, edition of Waterloo's *Semi-Weekly Courier* reported on a mysterious animal that was alarming farmers around Franklin County. The paper reported that the creature was a swine of some variety:

"What appears to be a wild hog, or an animal related to the hog species, is causing considerable excitement in this neighborhood at present.

"Parties hunting in Haynes' Grove for some time have been pursued and had their dogs chased by what seemed to be a vicious hog, and a number of our sportsmen have tried to get a shot at it, but without success.

"Monday night Theodore Thomas brought in two loads of hogs, which went out over the Central, and as it was late before he started to drive them in, darkness overtook him and his herd a short distance from his home.

"He had not proceeded far when his herd was attacked by a vicious animal of some kind which stampeded his herd, after maiming several fine animals. This attack was repeated several times before he reached town, each time his herd suffering.

"Mr. Thomas finally reached the stock yards at 10 p.m. and related the circumstance of the attack on his herd to a crowd in the pool room. Shortly after midnight residents in the neighborhood of the stock yards were aroused by the din of a terrible struggle. Trick Johnson and Gess Horner secured their shot guns and made for the yards, where they found a lean, but vicious animal in one of the alleys terribly punishing one of Mr. Thomas' hogs. Both men opened with their guns about the same time and after a few shots brought it down.

"The dead animal weighed 179 pounds. In appearance it resembled the hog species but differed in the enormous size of its tusks and great length of its bristles and its unusual length of legs.

"It is the opinion of many who have seen it at large as well as after death that it must have escaped from some show, as the animal was thoroughly vicious and never wintered in this country. The carcass is being held for investigation."

Phantom Kangaroo

August 4, 1999, started out like any other day for cattle rancher Lois Eckhardt, a resident of the town of Wellman in Washington County, that is, until she saw the odd animal on her property. Eckhardt told reporters that the creature "looked like a deer, but it had a bigger belly and a boxy nose and a long tail too long for a deer."

As the rancher watched, the animal "took off with a sort of long, low hop." The woman's descriptions made it obvious that she had spotted some kind of kangaroo, but what in the world was it doing out in rural Iowa?

Eckhardt kept quiet about the sighting, likely wondering if she had really seen the animal or not, but she piped in when another kangaroo was reported later in the month, on August 25.

This time, it was a Wapello County resident who spotted the animal. Mary Stangl of Ottumwa called the sheriff's office to report a kangaroo near her home.

Puzzled officials at the sheriff's office contacted local zoos to find out if they had lost a marsupial, but the facilities all reported that their kangaroos were present and accounted for. The rogue roos didn't spend much time in Iowa and if anyone else spotted them, they kept quiet about the matter.

Big Cats have been spotted prowling around Iowa

A Menagerie of Big Cats

Historical data shows that cougars once lived in the state of Iowa and records tell us that a number of them were killed by early pioneers in the state. John W. Laundre notes in his book *Phantoms of the Prairie: The Return of Cougars to the Midwest*:

"As late as the 1800s cougars were widely distributed across the state. It is unlikely though that they ever occurred in high numbers, except in the eastern part where there were extensive forested areas. The last one killed in the state was the one in 1867 from Appanoose County in south central Iowa."

Of course, this doesn't mean it was the last time a cougar was roaming around the Hawkeye State. For decades, stories of cougars, unidentified big cats, and phantom black panthers have cropped up in Iowa.

Frequently, a sighting or two, or even a handful, will be reported and then the matter is finished, likely the result of a transient mountain lion or other smaller known species being misidentified. Some sightings are more puzzling, however.

State officials are typically skeptical of big cat reports, stating simply that mountain lions aren't present in the state and that there's no such thing as black panthers. Yet, time and time again we see evidence that the big cats didn't get the memo that they aren't supposed to be around.

Some kind of big cat took up residence in a swamp in Polk County in 1890 and locals were "wild with excitement" according to Oxford Junction's *Mirror*.

The paper reported on the beast in its August 4 edition and said that the animal was making the "night hideous with its roaring."

Locals reported that the beast was near a creek that passed

through the farm of one George Powles. By all accounts, it was a nocturnal creature, and its voice was said to be "a cross between the roar of a lion and the screech of an enraged panther." The *Mirror* said the sound was terrifying:

"Several persons who, while walking or driving along the road near, have heard the roar, and becoming almost panic-stricken, cannot be induced to pass over the route again. One young man who, while accompanying a lady friend home recently, heard the appalling sound but a few yards distant, and being unarmed, rather than pass over the same route again, he made a detour of nearly ten miles to reach his home."

Locals were so concerned that they had reportedly organized a hunting party to track the beast down.

In its September 26, 1894, edition, Davenport's *Tribune* reported on the furor over some monstrous snakes that were reportedly on the loose in Hancock County. Blame for the reptiles was laid on Van Amberg's circus, a traveling menagerie that had purportedly lost the serpents in a wreck several years previous (see the giant snakes chapter in this book).

In the same report, the *Tribune* mentions that not only did the circus lose some of their snakes, but they also lost "two panthers and a litter of young."

The December 6, 1912, edition of Webster City's *Tribune* reported that a panther was causing trouble around Lorimer in Union County. According to the paper, residents of the area said that a big cat had lived in the woods around town for ten to fifteen years and made periodic appearances. It had been absent for some time but was suddenly active again. The animal's cries greatly disturbed locals who said the noise sounded like the scream of a woman.

An escaped leopard was reportedly roaming around Mills County in the fall of 1921. News sources said that the cat may have been one that had escaped from a Kansas City Zoo several weeks prior. Hull's *Sioux County Index* ran a piece on the cat, reporting the story from Glenwood:

"Several people the last week, while hunting along the Missouri River bottom near here report having seen an animal which they all describe as of the feline species and as big as a shepherd dog. Two who saw the strange animal declared it is a panther. Tracks of the animal have been followed and half dozen intrepid Glenwood men armed with shotguns and rifles took up the trail and followed it for many miles but lost it in the timber."

One of those non-existent black panthers showed up around Burlington in Des Moines County in the fall of 1946. One witness, Clifford E. Plumly, got a very clear view of the creature one night when it darted in front of him.

Around ten o'clock in the evening, Plumly was heading home after a visit with his nephew. He was driving toward Middletown gate when the animal appeared in the road in front of his car. Plumly told reporters with the *Hawk-Eye Gazette* (November 9, 1946, edition):

"I had to slam on the brakes to keep from running into it. I stopped the car about 20 feet from the animal and it looked right into the headlights. I'm certain it was a panther, its black fur glistened in the light."

Plumly said the animal was about five feet in length, had short legs and a bushy tail.

A month later, the *Hawk-Eye Gazette* was reporting on feline activity in neighboring Louisa County. According to the paper's December 28, 1946, edition, there were a pair of troublemakers this time—a black panther and its partner—a lion.

The paper announced that a mass hunt had been organized for New Year's Day to track the cats down.

Wapello resident Clayton Hartsock reported that his 150-pound coon dog had been mauled by "a full-grown male lion" during a night hunt. Hartsock said the cat had attacked him, too, and that he had only survived by smacking the lion on its head with the stock of his gun. Hartsock fell to his knees and the cat leapt over him and vanished in the darkness.

The hunter and his dog both survived the encounter, though the canine was badly clawed during the scuffle.

Around the same time, the Reverend R.J. Bloomquist,

Pastor of Wapello's Presbyterian church, saw a black panther on an area highway. Bloomquist told the paper:

"I saw a strange animal stalking toward me on the shoulder of the road. Its body was low to the ground, and noting that it was about 5 feet long, there was no doubt in my mind that it was a panther.

Walter Meredith, a gas station operator in Columbus Junction, organized a hunt and expected about a hundred men would join the New Year's search for the big cats.

As is inevitable, the paper soon pointed the blame at circus folk, stating:

"The beasts [are] thought by some persons to have been released by an itinerant showman last summer because of the meat shortage."

Yet another of those phantom panthers was reported in the January 7, 1947, edition of Burlington's *Hawk-Eye Gazette*.

Special game warden George Killinger was tracking the animal on the property of an area ordnance plant. Earl Welch, an agronomist with the plant, was with Killinger and the pair followed the animal for three miles in the snow.

Once they spotted it and got within shooting range, Killinger fired and killed the animal which turned out to be a forty-pound prairie wolf.

The hunt had been organized after two men—bus driver Darrell Wolfe and laborer Frank Wimler—reported a big cat on the loose. They were both on Wolfe's bus when they spotted a large creature lope across the road in front of the vehicle. They both claimed that it looked like a black panther.

The cat had been reported by others for about a year, so Killinger sought permission to track it down. He was convinced that the wolf he killed was the animal witnesses had spotted, though it's hard to imagine numerous people mistaking a wolf for a black panther.

The August 9, 1948, edition the *Muscatine Journal and News-Tribune* out of Muscatine, reported on a "mystery beast" prowling around Muscatine and Louisa counties. The creature had reportedly been lurking around the area for a year and a half. The animal was described as cat-like, five feet long, two to three feet in height, and dark in color with a smooth coat.

The animal showed up at the Holliday farm around ten miles outside Muscatine. Leonard Peterson spotted the beast when it was caught in the headlights of his car.

An area resident named Earl Harrison reported that he thought a neighbor's dog had fought the animal. The dog, a large German shepherd, returned from the woods badly mauled after having encountered something.

In the fall of 1948, a hunter named G.L. Thompson took a shot at a black panther that was about to leap and attack some pigs in Muscatine County. Thompson missed and the panther fled. The hunter said the animal was "coal black" and was a big specimen—about seven feet long by his calculations.

Thompson was led to the animal after finding unusual tracks that were approximately six inches in width. He followed the trackway and discovered the panther just before it jumped into the hog pen.

The November 12, 1948, edition of Waterloo's *Daily Courier* reported on the beast, noting that Muscatine County Sheriff Fred Nesper had led a posse of twenty men into the woods to track the animal down. The group searched around the area of Mad Creek where the panther had been sighted, but they came up empty handed. Authorities said they believed the panther was an escaped circus animal.

In October 1950, nineteen-year-old Paul Hildreth was trapped in a car for forty-five minutes while a black panther stalked around the vehicle, "roared" and put its paws up on the car.

Hildreth was working in some timberland on his father's property when he heard what he described as a "shrill scream." Scanning the area, he spotted a black panther on a nearby hill. The cat started toward Hildreth, so the man rushed to his car and jumped in for protection from the animal. Hildreth told reporters that the animal "put his paws on the car and roared," as if it were trying to get to him. The cat was likely frustrated by what it thought would be easy prey.

Mason City's *Globe-Gazette* reported on the incident from Polk County in its October 26 edition. The paper said that officials from the county sheriff's department were planning a hunt to search for the panther.

Hildreth's sister, Mrs. Anna May Cooley, said that other people in the area had reported seeing the panther over the summer. She said the creature was "coal black, 3 feet long and with a tail just as long."

Cooley also added that cattle had been killed in the area and the animal's bodies bore claw marks indicating a large, feline predator.

A second report of the panther soon came in. Robert Halterman of Des Moines was out hunting at Goodwin Lake southeast of Des Moines when he spotted a black panther up in a tree. Halterman told officials that the animal had a "black tail about the length of my arm." The panther was draped over some branches in the tree and its tail was hanging down.

Polk County sheriff Howard Reppert was on the hunt for the panther, and as reports hit the media, more attention was put on the matter. Officials in neighboring Warren County announced that they, too, would be launching a hunt for the beast in their area.

In mid-November T.L. (Mike) Lester reported that his 115-pound Tennessee boar-hunting dog had gotten into a fight with the big cat. Lester was out on a hunt when he encountered the cat. He described it as "a black, shiny animal with a long tail."

Lester said his dog had gone into a weed patch when "all hell broke loose. It was clear that his animal was doing battle with something, and Lester rushed in to see what was happening. The man was unarmed and when he got within thirty feet of the animal he started shouting at the thing. The noise was enough to cause the cat to run away from the scene. Lester's dog was badly mauled, but he reported that the animal was on the mend and would survive the encounter.

An *Associated Press* story from November 21, 1950, reported that the cat was causing a lot of trouble for locals and that the panther hunt was on. The story notes:

"Law enforcement officers, dogs and an airplane went on a 'safari' today to hunt down an elusive black beast that is giving northwest Des Moines the jitters.

"Several people have reported seeing the animal in the past several weeks and from their descriptions, officials said it could be a black panther. Tracks measuring about four inches across have been found.

"Kenneth Sunderleiter, who operates a zoo, warned people to beware. He said panthers sometimes attack people 'just for the sport of it.'"

By this time, officials were receiving countless phone calls from concerned citizens. They warned area residents to exercise caution when outside and suggested that parents use their own judgment in deciding whether to let their children go to school.

As locals grew more concerned, the hunt intensified. A

United Press story on November 21 announced that a civilian radio operator with the state's highway patrol had joined the hunt. Charles Austin was reportedly an "expert archer," and he suggested the best way to bring the cat down was with an arrow. Austin told reporters:

"On this type of hunt a bow and arrow would be an advantage because they create less shock than a bullet. The fire of a gun excites an animal and makes him mad, while an arrow doesn't."

One wonders if the cat would agree that being struck with an arrow is any better overall.

The frenzy over the wandering panther reached a new height of, well, stupidity when a mass of hunters crashed through the woods looking for the animal. Mason City's *Globe-Gazette* reported on the results in its November 21, 1950, edition under the headline: Posse Bags 1 Fox, 1 Hunter—No Panther." The story describes the chaotic, mass hunt:

"Orville Jones, 46, was hit in the mouth by stray shotgun pellets when a group of hunters opened up on what they thought was the mystery beast reportedly seen several times in the area about one mile northwest of Iowa's largest city.

"When the fox was sighted, the nearly 30 rifle-bearing members of the posse opened up with a barrage described by one reporter as 'like the Battle of the Bulge.'"

The poor fox was of course killed amidst the rain of bullets. Jones, the hunter who was hit, was taken to Des Moines hospital. He lost some teeth, but otherwise his condition was not serious. The paper reported how the incident had occurred:

"The hunters, armed with everything from pistols and shotguns to rifles with telescopic sights, closed in on the frightened fox when an airplane circling overhead began waggling its wings and diving frantically. A deputy in the plane reported by radio that he saw 'something.'"

On the ground, someone soon spotted movement and shouted that it was the beast and shots started to ring out. The whole fiasco was a clear example of why such mass "monster hunts" are a dangerous idea. The combination of tension, excitement, and lots of people crowded together with guns is a recipe for disaster and the group was fortunate that nothing worse happened.

Sheboygan, Wisconsin's, *Press-Telegram* was clearly unimpressed with the panther hunt and wrote about developments that had resulted from the mess. The paper's November 22, 1950, edition reported on the incident stating:

"[Deputy Sheriff Max] Van Rees said he would try to restrict the posse to a few hunters directed by a low flying plane. He called off yesterday's hunt after Jones, one of the task force of nimrods, was wounded by shotgun pellets in a wild round of firing at a hapless fox."

The *Press-Telegram* noted that the hunters had initially formed a long "skirmish line" for safety, but any semblance of order vanished as soon as someone reported seeing the animal.

The paper also reported on another panther sighting, this one at the farm of the Lockner family on the outskirts of Des Moines. Sheriff's deputies investigated the sighting and Mrs. Lockner reported:

"It was much too big for a dog, and certainly was not a cow. It resembled pictures of panthers I've seen."

The woman said the animal was long and shiny black in color. It was spotted darting through fields on the property. Officials at the scene discovered large cat-like tracks but did not attempt to track the beast.

Another farmer, this one in Urbandale, a suburb of Des Moines, also reported seeing the panther. Joe Woods called the sheriff's department and said a "shiny black animal with a long tail" was skulking around his stock farm. Woods was about thirty feet away from the creature and when it spotted the farmer, it took off.

The November 27, 1950, edition of Cedar Rapid's *Gazette* reported that Mrs. Laura Kimmel contacted the sheriff's department and told them that some hunters nearby had come across large tracks that appeared to be fresh in the same area that officials were scouring for the panther.

It was, for the most part, the last mention of the panther in the area at the time. It's likely for the best since the hunt for the animal had become dangerous and there were too many trigger-happy hunters roaming about.

The May 11, 1955, edition of the Iowa's *Postville Herald* ran a brief report on the search for a big cat:

"Lion Hunt—Two large scale lion hunts were held in the Correctionville area recently, after reports of a mysterious animal, believed to have been a mountain lion, were received. Nearly 200 persons took part in the hunt but bagged no lion."

In 1959 people in Hamburg, Freemont County, were reporting a big cat in their area, variously described as a black panther, mountain lion, or bobcat.

Clarence Hendrickson was out deer hunting near the Iowa / Missouri state line when he spotted the large cat. Hendrickson took a shot at the animal but missed and it ran off into the brush and vanished.

The December 3, 1959, edition of Glenwood's *Opinion-Tribune* reported that the animal was lurking somewhere near the Missouri River and that several area residents had seen it. "Only one thing is certain," the paper wrote, "a fairly large, black animal is now living on the bottoms west of Hamburg."

Northwest of Hamburg, the panther showed up near the home of Wayne Long. Long's son, Larry, was at home alone waiting for the rest of his family to get back from Hamburg. He was watching television when he heard a sound outside and investigated. The paper reports:

"He heard a scream similar to that of his exuberant younger sister and thought his parents were back. Turning on the yard light, he discovered the mysterious black beast standing 30 feet away in the drive. Larry rushed back inside for his gun, but the animal had disappeared when he came back outside."

Other residents in the area said they had heard childlike screams as well. Hunters out searching around the river bottoms discovered two and a half inch tracks but could not locate the animal.

Reportedly, a few weeks prior, a large black cat-like animal had been reported around Pacific Junction in Mills County. There was speculation that people around Hamburg were now dealing with the same beast.

A few sporadic reports of big cats surfaced in the 1970s in Iowa. An article in the Des Moines *Register* on April 28, 1974, discussed "alleged" mountain lion sightings in Iowa and mentioned the curious anecdote about a farmer who reported losing a calf to a "black cougar." Unfortunately, the report offered no further details.

An Iowa resident mentioned to me that a black panther was reportedly on the prowl around Council Bluffs in the late 1970s, but he could not offer details.

In his *Encyclopedia of Cryptozoology*, the late Michael Newton mentioned sightings in the same area in the summer of 1978. He reports that multiple witnesses reported the panther, though no further specifics are offered.

Another report sent to me (no original source listed) says that police officers discovered a two-month-old lion cub in Muscatine County in the fall of 1977. The animal was likely an exotic pet that had gotten loose, though officials were unable to locate the owner.

People in Clarke County were stirred up over panther reports in the spring of 1992. Des Moines's *Register* reported on the predator in its May 2 edition. Reporters spoke with area resident Steve Carney who said the cat had broken the neck of a 150-pound pregnant ewe on his property. The beast dragged the carcass ten feet to an open area where it ate flesh from its victim's neck and ribs. It also carried away one of the animal's legs when it left the scene. Carney said the attack had occurred about March 1 and it wasn't the only attack in the area.

On April 22, a hundred-pound calf was attacked in a pasture. Other livestock was also attacked and torn apart. Claw marks were visible on the carcasses of the slain animals. Craig Roberg, state conservation officer for Clarke and Decatur counties, investigated the scene of the calf slaughter. He stated:

"It appears to me from the pattern of claw marks on the calf that it was a cougar."

Roberg noted that several big cat reports had come in from the two counties for several years and he believed that the animal was an exotic pet that had been set loose.

A Menagerie of Big Cats

Giant Snakes

A variety of snake species live in Iowa, including the common garter snake, the colorful smooth green snake, the redbelly snake, and the multi-colored milk snake. There are venomous species, too, including the prairie rattlesnake, the eastern massasauga rattlesnake, and the copperhead. Of course, these are normal sized serpents that have been chronicled and catalogued, but according to legend, some much larger specimens may have cropped up over the years. Some of these accounts cross into water monster territory, but perhaps that's just the nature of such large, slithering things.

In 1880, the Des Moines River was said to be the abode of a giant snake, twenty to thirty feet in length, and between eight and ten inches in diameter. Sightings of the creature were centered around Webster City, Hamilton County. The *Herald* out of Dubuque reported on the hunt for the serpent in its August 21 edition:

"There is much excitement in the neighborhood over the appearance of this monster snake, and a large party of men are in the woods today endeavoring to find and destroy it. Yesterday it was traced into what is supposed to be its den—a large, cavernous opening in a ledge of rocks on the riverbank.

According to the *Herald* the snake had been seen a few days prior to the hunt a few miles from the property of H. Ross.

A couple of months later, people around Moulton in Appanoose County were talking about a giant snake seen in their community. One Dr. C.D. Brown reportedly captured the snake and said that it was likely a native of Africa.

Burlington's *Weekly Hawk Eye* reported on the snake in its October 14, 1880, edition. Surprise, surprise, they speculated that the snake had escaped from a traveling circus. Rather than a vague allegation against some unknown menagerie, the paper did offer specifics on this occasion. According to the report, a man named Robert Allison was the original owner of a large cage of snakes that he displayed in a circus managed by George Cramer. Allison traveled with the circus in 1879, keeping an unlisted number of snakes in a cage together with a crocodile. According to the *Hawk Eye*:

"Allison carried these reptiles with Cramer's circus and exhibited them in a sideshow. Somewhere between Webster City and Fort Dodge, Allison being behind, his cage was overturned and broken in, and all the reptiles made their escape. The crocodile was afterwards retaken, but the snakes were never seen again."

"Snakes as big as logs" were causing concern in Davenport, Scott County in the fall of 1894. You'll be shocked to hear that Davenport's *Tribune* blamed the incidents on a traveling circus.

According to the paper's September 26, 1894, edition, the snakes had escaped while Van Amberg's circus was traveling through the area on the way to Carthage. A storm had come in and the circus folk had closed up quickly to try to beat the incoming wind and rain. The event had occurred "several years ago" according to the paper.

The *Tribune* added plenty of drama to the tale, reporting that a caravan of wagons from the circus was crossing the Crooked Creek bottoms when "the storm broke forth in its fury." As a result, two large boa constrictors escaped from their cages and made their way into the water.

(For good measure, the report also stated that a pair of panthers and a litter of their young had also escaped).

No one knew how large the snakes were, although the paper warned that "showmen say the snakes were monsters and had not yet attained their full size."

Hunters and fishermen who had been reporting strange creatures in the water around the area dismissed the idea that the creatures were escaped circus snakes. According to the tales, the things were larger than normal snakes of any breed and more closely resembled sea serpents. The paper said that the common opinion was that the creature, or creatures, had "come up from the Illinois River."

A man named George Washington Billstein saw the serpent for himself one evening around six o'clock. Billstein was near the Crooked Creek bottoms when he saw what he first took to be a large, hollow log on the road ahead. He was puzzled because he had travelled the route earlier in the day and the object wasn't here.

Billstein suddenly realized that the object was a living creature—a massive snake. The man's horses snorted in fright and reared. As Billstein watched, he received another surprise. As the paper reports:

"The great reptile began to uncoil itself yards at a time until, GW declares, the woods seemed to be full of snake. The air was filled with a deadening odor that made pioneer Billstein sick at the stomach. No sooner had Billstein got a good focus upon this monster than from a neighboring thicket came another large snake and the air was filled with hisses that heat a dozen locomotive explosions."

Billstein got control of his panicked horses, turned them around, and retreated from the scene, making his way to another road, and taking a longer route home in order to bypass the massive serpents. He told his neighbors about the snakes and, returning to the spot, the group discovered "great trails in the soft earth" and young trees and brush that had been beaten into the ground. The snakes themselves were nowhere to be found.

A year later, Davenport citizens were again stirred up by tales of a massive snake in their area. According to reports, the creature was fourteen feet long with a body as big around as a pail. The snake's head was diamond-shaped and capped with a "crest shaped like a crown."

The unusual creature was spotted by several prominent members of the community. According to the September 7, 1895, edition of the Davenport *Daily Tribune*:

"The monster was first seen about three weeks ago by Justice Veltor. Since then, it has been seen at intervals by I.W.

Valentine, superintendent of the Baptist Union Sunday School, and by Dr. Oliver Jones. The latter chased the snake into the woods in an effort to capture it but was unsuccessful."

Area residents were calling the creature the "king of snakes" and were worried that it would attack people, so they were anxious to kill or capture it. However, no further updates were reported, and the snake may have slithered away to parts unknown.

According to the September 29, 1885, edition of the *Burlington Hawk-Eye* out of Burlington, Iowa, locals were worried about a large serpent spotted in their area. The snake was purportedly harassing a community "across the river." The paper reported:

"A Kirkwood man who saw it some days ago says it is about forty feet long, thick as a young tree, makes a track in the dust the width of a man's two hands, and raises its head up four or five feet as it travels, with tongue protruding a yard in length and emitting a sound like the roaring of a train of cars." The paper notes that the creature had been reported in the area twenty-five years prior.

The *Humeston New Era* reported in its August 8, 1888, edition that a monster snake had been discovered along the Chariton River. The beast was reported to be twenty feet in length, though no further details were offered.

The *New York Times* ran an article about an Iowa monster in its October 1, 1893, edition. Despite the headline proclaiming "A Sea Serpent in Iowa," the article recounts details of a monster snake, though it is one purportedly living in the water. The paper made a point to mention that a Methodist minister was vouching for the veracity of the snake story.

Sightings of the creature began in the summer when farmers around the town of Scranton in Green County started reporting a giant snake preying on their hogs. It was believed that the creature had made its way up the Mississippi River, and theories suggested it had possibly come from the Gulf of Mexico before settling in the country around Scranton.

The troubles in the area began when one farmer, Jacob

Black, started losing hogs. Black's property was ten miles out of town and his hogs had been swiped from the pasture he had them in. His first thought was that a gang of thieves were at work, but the culprit was revealed when a neighbor crossing over Black's property saw one of the hogs being taken. The *Times* reported:

"He was startled by hearing a hog squeal, and, looking up, saw a hog that would weigh about 200 pounds in a coil of the snake and the hog lifted seven or eight feet from the ground.

"The man for an instant was paralyzed, as he was only about forty steps from the serpent. The snake seemed to pay no attention to the man, but after smashing the life out of the hog, very leisurely wended his way to the river and went over the bank into the same."

Another area farmer soon reported that he had also seen the serpent. Allie Griffee claimed the creature wasn't alone—it was surrounded by a horde of younger ones.

Griffee was bolder than the first witness. Reportedly, he waited for the large snake to move away, then swept in and killed a couple of the smaller snakes. They were eight feet in length and covered with small scales similar to those of a fish, but smaller.

A party of hunters out searching for the massive serpent found that it was living in a hole in the high riverbank. On inspection, they discovered several holes that were being used by the creature, all about ten inches in diameter. The snake, it seemed, had a whole network of holes along the riverbank and as the men watched, it slithered in and out, sometimes parts of the snake could be seen at multiple holes at the same time.

One of the men took a shot at the beast, but this only seemed to anger it. According to the *Times* article, the snake responded by leaving the area:

"He lifted his head high into the air and whistled so shrilly that it sent terror to the hearts of the bravest, and all fled in confusion. They heard an awful splashing in the water and then the whistling ceased.

"They describe the monster as being at least forty feet in length. They say his head is about the size of a calf's head and the body in the largest places about ten inches in diameter."

Word about the giant snake attracted more people who turned out at the riverbank while a company of men excavated the holes along the river searching for the creature. The snake didn't appear to be on the scene, but when the men dug into the creature's pit, they discovered bones of hogs, cattle, and a portion of a young colt.

"A reporter, anxious to get a glimpse of the snake, sauntered down the bank of the river 200 yards, when to his right he heard a strange noise, and on looking up he saw, hanging from a huge elm limb, this great, slimy monster. The reporter beat a hasty retreat and was hotly pursued by the snake and would have been crushed had it not been for Mantie Pattin, who appeared just in time and fired two charges of shot into the snake, which sent him whistling like a steam engine into the river."

In 1907, a man on horseback claimed he was chased by a twelve-foot-long serpent near Steamboat Rock in Hardin

County. The September 23 edition of Waterloo's *Daily Courier* carried the bizarre story and reported:

"There has been a monster snake which has been crawling its slimy length through the Van Note pasture, near Steamboat Rock. Lynn Ruby, who has the pasture leased, was the latest person to come in contact with the monster a few days since.

"He was riding a pony rounding up some cattle he had in the pasture, when all at once looking over a ravine to the hillside beyond a short distance he saw the snake, which he describes as probably twelve feet in length, from six to eight inches in diameter with head erect, coming with all possible speed toward him. After taking a good view of the reptile he concluded he did not care to make battle with him, especially since he had no suitable weapon for successful snake extermination, and turned his pony's head in the opposite direction and putting the spur to him made all possible haste to leave the 'critter' behind him in the pasture, although it followed him a considerable distance ere it ceased to give him chase.

"Ruby says the snake, which he thinks had a head broader than the back of a good-sized man's hand, continued to hiss as it followed him."

A farm in Randall, Hamilton County, was the focal point of a giant snake report in 1909. This creature was said to be a startling 25 to 30 feet in length.

Waterloo's *Daily Reporter* ran a story on the giant in its June 11, 1909, edition. The snake, the paper said, was active on farmland a half mile east of town.

M.L. Henderson and his hired hand, Geo. Anfinson, were at work plowing fields on what they thought would be a normal working day. Anfinson couldn't believe his eyes when a massive snake slid across an area of freshly plowed ground. The creature's size was alarming and Anfinson rushed over the hillside to find Henderson and report the sighting.

Despite some distance, Henderson could see the trail left by the serpent and sent for a gun and his dog. While the two men waited to be armed, they scanned the countryside. Looking in the direction that the snake had gone, the men saw a herd of cattle grazing near a large tree. The cattle suddenly became alarmed at something and stampeded. Henderson's gun and dog arrived, and the men set off to track the serpent. The men followed the trail to the spot where the cattle had been grazing and beyond that, down to the banks of the Skunk River where the trail vanished.

The men found an area nearby where the snake appeared to have been lying, a spot frequented by chickens belonging to Henderson's neighbor, H.G. Pederson.

Pederson himself reported that he had often seen the large trail left by the serpent, but he didn't know what the track was from since he hadn't seen the snake itself.

The story in the *Reporter* noted that the tracks were "larger than the track left by the largest automobile wheel…about eight inches in width."

Anfinson reportedly spotted the massive snake again later the same day when he was back at work plowing the field.

The paper assures us that Henderson and Anfinson were of the "best standing" in the community so there was no question of the truth of the tale.

Traveling menageries were blamed yet again when a giant snake showed up along the Cedar River near Waterloo in 1911.

The creature was supposed to be 18 to 20 feet in length and rather aggressive. According to the June 29 edition of Nashua's *Reporter*, a pair of young men out canoeing spotted the creature which "appeared to be very hungry and lashed its tail in a menacing way." The men, the paper noted, were involved in temperance work, an implication that the account was factual and not the result of alcoholic delusions.

The paper also reported a sighting from several years prior (date not given) involving a man named Harry Piersol of Cedar Falls. Piersol was fond of boating and was on the river one night when he had a frightening encounter. The paper reports:

"One night Mr. Piersol went alone for a ride and was paralyzed by the horrible vision that met his gaze. A few rods away he noticed a commotion in the water and was astounded to see the head of a huge reptile emerge. It kept coming up and up until about 10 feet of the snake was in the air.

"With the hideous and massive head weaving back and forth with fire flashing from the eyes and with an immense tongue blood red darting in and out of a mouth as large as an alligator's, Mr. Piersol nearly broke his oars so rapidly did he row away. He does not know how long the reptile was, but it must have been thirty or forty feet judging from the area of the river that was lashed into foam."

Residents around the town of Imogene, Fremont County, were reportedly "in the throes of excitement" in the fall of 1913 due to the presence of a massive python that was roaming the country.

Perry, IA's *Daily Chief* reported on the snake in its September 13, 1913, edition. Railroad men working on the west division of the Milwaukee reported the incidents, noting that the accounts had been circulating for a week. Citizens of Imogene had spotted the serpent's trail on dusty roads in the area and the large size of the track had people stirred up. The news reported:

"A few days ago, Mike Doyle, Jr., saw the snake itself and gives a minute description of the reptile. He says it stretched clear across the road, its head far in the brush on one side and its tail hidden in the weeds on the other side of the road. Its body was about 5 inches thick, and its color was black and yellow."

Doyle reported that the snake was about fourteen feet in length and said it was too large for him to attack since he wasn't armed. "Nobody ought to meet that snake unless armed with a Winchester rifle," Doyle stated.

The *Chief* reported that a party was being organized to hunt the snake down since there was concern it would start feeding on local farm animals. The paper referred to the snake as a python, though there seems to be no further detail offered as to the creature's identity or origin. Surprisingly, no one blamed a circus, but the paper did state that the news was "the best snake story in Iowa" for the year.

Fairfield, Iowa's *Daily Ledger* ran a giant snake account in its October 2, 1939, edition. Under the banner "Snake Story Told by Early Hunter," the paper detailed an account submitted by a man who preferred to remain anonymous, but he "vouched for it being absolutely true." The correspondent reported:

"One year in the early spring while out hunting, one of the early settlers of Jefferson County came upon the edge of a large swamp. The bank at this place was several feet high. Crawling up so he could see over the bank and not be seen, the hunter waited patiently for some ducks to come in. While waiting there, he was suddenly startled by a commotion in the water. Rising to his feet, holding his gun in his hand in readiness for instant use, a strange sight met his eyes.

"Out in the swamp was a large serpent or snake about twenty feet long, which had a duck in its mouth. The serpent, seeing the hunter on the bank, started to swim rapidly toward him; the hunter, thinking the serpent was making after him, cocked his gun and when the reptile drew nearer, fired both barrels into its body, without seeing effect. The serpent kept coming toward him at a terrific speed. It looked as if he would surely run head foremost into the steep bank but imagine the hunter's surprise when the snake seemed to pierce the earth and enter right into the solid bank, disappearing, leaving only a blood-stained trail behind.

"After picking up courage, the hunter decided to see where the serpent had gone and found a hole just at the water's edge where it had entered. Whether it died from the effects of the gunshot or not he was never able to find out, but this was the first and only time that he saw this strange reptile."

Giant Snakes

MONSTERS OF THE HAWKEYE STATE by David Weatherly

Humanoid Monsters

Phantom cats, kangaroos and giant snakes obviously fall into the animal section of the weirdness category, but there's even more strangeness to be found in Iowa lore—monsters of a more humanoid variety. Some are fantastical such as legends of giant humans; others are, well, more unsettling as we shall see.

MONSTERS OF THE HAWKEYE STATE by David Weatherly

Giants

Legends of giants are found far and wide and Iowa history has some curious news items related to purported massive humans, or rather, their remains.

Camden, New Jersey's *Courier-Post* covered the news that a giant had been found in Burlington, Iowa, in the summer of 1897. The paper's August 17 edition reported that workmen excavating for a road on North Main Street had made the discovery. The skeletons were complete and included an adult and infant. The adult was "at least seven feet tall." A spear head, silver armlet, knives, beads, and other assorted items were found buried with the remains.

The November 19, 1897, edition of the *Nebraska Advertiser* reported on the find of a giant in an Iowa mound that measured seven feet six inches in height. According to the paper, the bones "crumbled to dust when exposed to the air" so other details were scant. Scientists reportedly found several items in the burial, including a bear tooth collar and a hunting skirt with dozens of small copper beads.

Another giant report surfaced the same year, this one in the December 25 edition of the *Omaha Daily Bee*.

The article reports on the opening of a burial mound in Southeastern Iowa in which many artifacts and a giant skeleton were found. According to the Bee:

"One remarkable skeleton was dug up by myself and another man. It was that of a giant, being over seven feet six inches in height. An idea of the size of this man may be gained by the length of his shin bone. I stood it on the ground at my heel and it reached about two inches above my knee joint, being twenty-five inches in length. The only part of the skeleton we were able to take away was the jawbone. Everyone who has seen it says it is the most massive jaw ever seen by them. It measures from the top of the front teeth to the lower edge of the jawbone one- and three-quarter inches. Around the lower edge it measures six and a half inches; across the jaw from the two tips is five and a half inches. It has a remarkably perfect set of teeth.

Iowa's *Clinton Mirror* reported on the find of a giant skeleton in its April 28, 1900, edition. According to the paper, the bones were discovered on the banks of the Iowa River in Hardin County. The location was noted as six miles north of Eagle City (now a ghost town) and was believed to be related to the mound builders. The paper reports:

"Although well preserved, it is estimated that the skeleton is centuries old. The skull is very large and thick, fully a quarter of an inch. A set of almost round double teeth are remarkably well preserved. They are yellow with age, are perfect in shape and appear to have been double, both above and below. The femurs are very long, showing a giant in stature."

A physician, Dr. N.C. Morse, reportedly examined the bones and was impressed by them. The skeleton was reportedly displayed for some time in a shop window in the town of Eldora though no one seems to know what became of them afterwards.

Even stranger perhaps is a headline in the September 13, 1900, edition of Buffalo, New York's *Buffalo Review* which proclaimed, "Discovery of Bones of a Race of Monkey Men."

The article reported on the discovery of fourteen giant skeletons in mounds in Chickasaw County, Iowa. Archaeologist Professor Clement L. Webster had made the find and was at work excavating the site, located on the west side of the Little Cedar River. The paper reports:

"The mounds are from two to five feet apart, are circular, round-topped and measure from twenty-two to fifty-one feet in diameter and from one and three-fourths to five feet in height. The main line of mounds runs north, and a few degrees east. The others run parallel to the main line."

The mounds had been graded down substantially over the

years, and at the time of the find, the land was owned by R.H. Gordon who had been farming it.

The skeletons were found in sitting positions, some facing each other, and at least one of the mounds was empty. The skeletons were very unusual. The *Review* described the skeletons:

"Fourteen well preserved skeletons of a race whose skulls are almost flat on the crown and whose forearms compare favorably in length with the legs, adding to the belief that these peoples in their life could scamper along on all-fours at a lively and natural gait."

The paper went on to theorize about a lost race of monkey men:

"His long arms may have assisted him in swinging from tree to tree when pursued by fierce animals, as it is held by men of knowledge that men in the earliest states had no weapons of defense except what nature provided."

The lost race of monkey men has apparently remained lost since nothing further seems to have come of the story. Given the time period, the tale may have been completely fabricated, or it could have been a wild exaggeration of mound excavations in the region.

Another tale that has been passed around extensively on various online sites claims that the mummies of seven giants were uncovered in Kossuth County.

Reportedly, the mummies were found in a stone tomb similar to something the Egyptians would have built. The site was located on the property of a farmer named Marvin Rainwater.

The mummies were ten feet tall and had red hair, low, sloping foreheads and prominent brows. They also bore double rows of teeth in both the upper and lower jaws.

There are numerous problems with the account, the first and foremost being that the original source of the story is difficult to find. Some sources claim the account was from an early newspaper, while others say the discovery of the tomb occurred in recent years.

The Spring 2003 issue of the *Iowa Historian,* official newsletter of the State Historical Society of Iowa, reported that Dan Higginbottom, an archeologist with the society, had received an email asking him about the purported giants. Higginbottom, a man who had been involved in archeology in the Midwest for twenty years, had never heard the tale before, a good indication of its recent providence and likely fabrication.

Bigfoot researcher Ray Crowe related a report from a 1917 edition of the *Chillicothe Weekly Constitution* that stated a thirty-pound petrified foot had been discovered in Webster County. The object was found by miners working a coal mine near Lehigh. It measured over two feet long. Crowe notes that at 6 ½ inches per foot length, the being would have been thirteen feet tall.

Giant humans are one thing, but some legends in the Hawkeye State speak of even weirder creatures.

Giants

MONSTERS OF THE HAWKEYE STATE by David Weatherly

Iowa Vampire

Did a vampire once plague Woodbury County? If the article in the April 25, 1895, edition of the *Illustrated Police News* is true there was, or at least, there was someone who acted like one of the traditional bloodsuckers. A wealthy rancher name Converse was the creature's unfortunate victim. The publication reported:

"There is a maniac confined in the Sioux City Lunatic Asylum who imagines himself a vampire and is considered excessively dangerous. A close watch was kept over him, but he managed to elude the vigilance of the guards and escaped on Wednesday morning. Not long afterwards he met Mr. Converse on the high road. He sprang at him in a fury, bore Converse to the ground, and literally tore him to pieces with his teeth. When Converse ceased to struggle the maniac fastened on his neck and sucked the blood from a gaping wound. He then returned to the asylum, where his shocking appearance showed the asylum officials that something dreadful had happened. Search was made, when the mangled body of the maniac's victim was discovered, mutilated almost beyond recognition."

As if a vampire isn't enough, Iowa also has a werewolf legend and it's more modern than the bloodsucking tale.

Iowa Vampire

MONSTERS OF THE HAWKEYE STATE by David Weatherly

Werewolves

In Webster County, just outside of Fort Dodge, there's an old bridge that has some curious legends associated with it. The spot is somewhat hard to find, sitting amidst the secluded, former town of Tara. The bridge is said to be haunted by the spirits of young children who were killed by their own mother. The ghosts of these children are purportedly troublesome and people who journey to the area at night claim that you can hear the kids screaming. It's also claimed that vehicles traveling over the bridge will suddenly shut off.

My friend and colleague Chad Lewis mentions the bridge in his book *The Iowa Road Guide to Haunted Locations* (co-written with Terry Fisk).

Lewis and Fisk note that the town of Tara was platted in 1883 and Tara Junction and Tara Station were constructed in 1893. For many years, the area has purportedly been a spot for weird activity, due not just to the reported spectral children, but other manifestations as well. Since the 1800s, people have reported being chased through the area by a "mysterious, howling ghost rider."

Bernice Hicks and Ruby Woodbury mention the bridge's legends in the *Douglas Township Historical Story*. According to the authors, an early tragedy in the area may have started the legends:

"The story goes that several farmers were in the fields haying when a fierce wind picked up, making it extremely difficult to work. One man flippantly cursed the wind in hopes that it would settle down and the men could go back to work. However, he was not so lucky…as no sooner than the words left his mouth, he fell to the ground dead."

If curses, ghost children and phantom riders aren't enough, there's one more addition to his bizarre collection at the bridge—a werewolf.

In his book *Our Lizard Creek Farm*, author Ray Flaherty mentions this strange figure:

"One summer the rumor got around that there was a wild man living in our woods, seeking shelter from the rains either underneath the trees or under the railroad bridge."

Flaherty's mention is brief and could be explained away if it were the only incident, but it's not. Lewis and Fisk mention another account, originally reported by Deann Haden Luke:

"A woman, her son, and a friend were traveling near Tara when they encountered an extremely large wild animal that ran past them at a high rate of speed. They were able to get a good look at the creature when it ran directly in front of them. What baffled the witness was that the creature was running on its hind legs."

I was told a similar story myself by a young man who said that as a teenager he and two friends had gone out to the bridge on a dare. Just as the sun was starting to set, the trio spotted a bipedal creature with pointed ears and a long snout. "I don't want to say it was a werewolf," the man reported, "because it just sounds so crazy, but that was not a natural creature."

The creature ran off and the boys sped away from the area and never returned.

An even more bizarre tale comes from Chad Lewis who spoke with a woman about her experience at the bridge. The woman told Chad that she and some friends took a ride out to see the haunted bridge. As they were slowly driving away from the area, they noticed a "werewolf looking creature running parallel to them on the grassy side of the road." The driver panicked at the sight and hit the gas to race away from the thing.

"Even as they hit 50 mph on the gravel road, the creature kept up with them as though it was a walk in the park," said Lewis.

As if the tale wasn't weird enough, there was another strange element to the tale, an element that initially made the woman very reluctant to share her account at all. She told Lewis:

"The creature was wearing a plaid suit jacket like an old professor at a university might wear. After a few moments of racing the vehicle, the beast simply disappeared from view."

Even if some of the tales are mere legend, it seems that Tara Bridge, often referred to as "Terror Bridge," is a focal point of high strangeness.

A report filed with the BFRO about an incident in Sac County sounds to me more like a dogman sighting than a Bigfoot encounter. The sighting took place in July 2013 on a country road in a rural area southwest of the town of Auburn.

Four witnesses were traveling in a vehicle. The reporting witness was sitting in the back seat. It was between ten p.m. and midnight when a "very big, black, hairy animal" crossed the road in front of the vehicle. The witness reported:

"It had a very arched back...its strides were strange. The face was sort of dog-like, but it was hard to see it real good in detail because it was dark."

The witness added that the creature's legs were "bent back," and that even on four legs, it was taller than the car and bigger than a horse. The thing crossed the road in a couple of steps.

The witness states that the same creature had been seen by other locals in 2005, and that two to three years prior to his own report, his brother had seen the thing. Reportedly, his brother was driving on a gravel road near the town of Early (also in Sac County) when he spotted a black hairy animal in a ditch. As the driver got closer, the creature seemed to react to the vehicle's approach:

"The strange creature stood up on its hind legs just [a] little taller than [the] full grown corn; it was summer. The creature had pointy ears." It was the most frightening thing he had seen in his life.

The driver raced home and once he arrived, he learned that his girlfriend, who had been following him, had also seen the creature. According to the girl, the thing got down on all fours and crossed the road. She reported being extremely frightened by the sight of the creature.

Werewolves

Weird Humanoids

A weird "fire man" was seen in Davenport, Scott County. The report, dated July 15, 1885, is, at the least, quite puzzling. Jerome Clark dug the account up and published it on the *Magonia Exchange Project*. The case involves a family named Richardson and begins early one morning when the family's youngest daughter ran to a neighbor's house in a panic. She said that a "huge man all covered with fire" had entered the family's home and carried everyone else away.

The neighbors assumed that the Richardson farm was on fire, so they rushed out to offer aid. Reaching the home, they found no flames but no people either.

The house was empty, but nothing was disturbed. The family's horse and buggy were in the stable and the inside of the home looked completely normal. A thorough search was made of the area, but no signs of the Richardsons could be found, and locals were puzzled as to where the family had gone.

Another family moved into the house, intending to watch over both it and the young girl until the Richardsons returned. The new residents reported strange goings on in the home, including a bright white light that filled the house, and the voice of Mr. Richardson calling out to his daughter even though he was nowhere to be seen. When the young girl responded to her father, a "great shower of small stones fell upon the roof."

The poltergeist-like activity at the home reportedly went on for some time, but the mystery of the Richardsons disappearance never seems to have been resolved, nor does the question of the strange "fire man."

Brad Steiger was a well-known author and explorer of all things strange. Steiger wrote numerous books on the ghosts,

UFOs, spirituality, and associated fields.

Steiger himself had some strange experiences throughout his life. In his book *Starborn*, co-written with his wife Sherry Hansen Steiger, Brad tells the story of an odd entity he saw when he was a young boy living on a farm in the Des Moines area.

One October night in 1940, Brad heard what he thought was someone walking around outside his bedroom window. Since the home was in the country, two miles east of town, it was unlikely that person was walking outside the house.

Brad then heard a tin washtub being dragged from the well outside. The boy was now curious about the sounds and wondered why Bill, the family dog, had not sounded the alarm. He went to the window and peered outside. As recounted in *Starborn*:

"He was astonished by the sight of a smallish man settling the tub beneath the kitchen window that was directly opposite his bedroom. Bill crouched beside the stranger completely mute, as if transfixed."

Brad's mother and father were in the kitchen and the light from the room window spilled out from the house onto the figure.

"The kitchen curtain was open, and the light from the lamp illuminated the little man's head and upper body as he raised himself on tiptoes to peer in at Brad's mother and father. Brad could clearly see his disproportionately large head, two pointed ears, and long, slender fingers as they grasped the windowsill.

As the figure was staring in at Brad's parents, it somehow sensed that it was being observed by the boy. The humanoid turned its face toward young Brad. Enormous, slanted eyes with vertical, reptilian-like pupils stared at the boy. Young Steiger felt a hypnotic effect and the next thing he recalled, the entity was gone, and it was morning.

Perhaps Steiger's encounter was of the alien variety, but the description of reptilian-like eyes cast a more earthly, sinister shadow on the account.

Famed UFO investigator Dr. J. Allen Hynek received details of incidents near the town of Elkader in Clayton County where a farmer and his pregnant wife reported having encounters with a range of unearthly beings on their property in October 1969. The entities ranged in height from very small—two to five feet—to very large—ten feet.

On one level, the accounts sound like typical sensational space man fare of the period but it wasn't just the single couple reporting the incidents, a number of families in both Clayton and neighboring Allamakee County said they were dealing with the creatures.

On at least one occasion, a number of beings were present, ranging from two feet up to five feet in height. The five-foot-tall creatures wore black belts that offered some kind of protective force field. One farmer reportedly threw a tree branch at the entities, but the wood exploded in mid-air before it struck them.

The ten-foot-tall creatures were reportedly very hostile and were able to issue fire from the soles of their boots.

In the summer of 1970, two men encountered some kind of humanoid near the Mississippi River. Check Henderson, a tractor trailer driver, was taking an evening walk in June with a friend named Walter Harlock. The pair had strolled to a field known as Bulger's Hollow close to the river. The area was around four to five miles from the town of Clinton in Clinton County.

Their walk was disrupted by the appearance of a six-foot-tall creature with a large head, glowing red eyes, and a slit for a mouth. "We had a head-on confrontation after the being walked up the riverbank and stood facing us at a distance of about ten feet," Henderson reported.

A report on the incident in the publication Pursuit (issue #62) notes that the creature was "broad-shouldered, had dark, dull gray skin of a scaly nature, and appeared to weigh about 250 pounds."

The witnesses reported that the creature stood looking at them for approximately one minute, then quickly scampered down an embankment and vanished into the trees along the river.

Another bizarre figure showed up in the summer of 1974 outside the town of Madrid in Boone County. A report from researcher Albert Rosales relates the details of the incident.

Three men, Sidney Phipps, Ron Weaver, and Paul Talk were sitting in a vehicle on a bridge west of town. It was early evening and the men noticed what appeared to be a humanoid figure across the field on another bridge. Strangely, the man-like being was glowing.

The witnesses reported that the man glowed from top to bottom and the pure, white light was unlike anything they had ever seen before. The figure saw the men watching it and it began moving toward them. The three witnesses exited their car and started moving toward the figure themselves.

The glowing humanoid started calling out to the men in a "high-pitched, modulate tone" and the men could not understand what the entity was saying. The sound was extremely loud, and the men started shouting back at the figure. At this, the entity responded, as the report notes:

"The figure suddenly stopped, turned, and ran under the bridge. By the time the men reached the area where it had run off into, they saw a large, glowing ball flying away from the area at high speed. It shot towards the southwest and disappeared."

In their book *Haunted: Malevolent Ghosts, Night Terrors, and Threatening Phantoms*, Brad and Sherry Steiger shared a story related to them by a former classmate of Brad's.

Brad notes that he grew up in a small Iowa community that was almost one hundred percent Scandinavian American, with a few German American Roman Catholic families thrown in the mix.

Steiger tells the story of a woman he calls Clarice, an especially devout young lady who longed to be a Lutheran pastor. Unfortunately for her, growing up in the 1940s and 50s, such a thing wasn't possible—the church at the time only accepted male clergy. Clarice, Steiger reports, ended up marrying a college professor and went to work as a librarian at a church.

Years later, when the Steigers were living in Phoenix, AZ, they got to visit with Clarice when she visited from the Midwest. It was during the visit that the woman shared an extraordinary tale.

Knowing that the Steigers wrote about unusual encounters and events, Clarice said she had a story to tell that she could no longer contain.

Her story was from her early life, living on her parents' farm in rural Iowa. When she was home alone, Clarice would often go out to a grove on the property, climb up on a tree trunk, and practice giving a sermon, imagining herself as a minister.

Late one afternoon the girl was practicing one such sermon when she noticed a rustling in the bushes near her. What happened next stayed with the woman all her life. As the Steigers write:

"Before her disbelieving eyes, she beheld strange and hideous creatures emerging from behind trees and under fallen trees, and also from peculiar holes in the ground. Their faces were grotesque, resembling reptiles the likes of which did not slither through Iowa fields. Their voices made horrible, grating, growling sounds."

Clarice realized that the hideous little creatures were moving toward the tree she was in and starting to surround the trunk. It was as if they had sensed her presence and come out of their holes to come after her. She told the Steigers that when the creatures opened their mouths, she could see fangs and long tongues. Clarice knew she had to escape the things, so she leapt down from the tree and ran for home.

She told Brad and Sherry that the creatures only pursued her to the edge of the grove where the sunlight seemed to stop them. Brad adds:

"The story, admittedly, will border on the fantastic to many, but I have known Clarice since I was five years old. Not once did I ever hear her recount some wild and crazy story. In fact, I don't think I ever heard her tell a joke. And not in a hundred years could I imagine her telling a lie."

A woman living in Elkader, in Clayton County, spotted a "stick man" on her farm on February 15, 2004. It was around 11:00 p.m. and the woman was walking back to her house after some late-night chores. She was almost at her door when something to her left caught her eye. She turned to see a "thing" that she could only describe as a "stick man" running very quickly about thirty yards from her position.

As the figure ran, it turned its head, looking over its left shoulder and straight at the witness. It then started running toward the woman who quickly rushed inside her home and locked all her doors.

According to the NUFORC (National UFO Reporting Center) report, it took two hours for the woman to calm down after the experience. She believed the entity wanted her to see it, but she was at a loss as to why or what the thing really was.

A writer and adventure guide had a bizarre encounter with some kind of humanoid in Maquoketa Caves State Park in mid-June 2017.

Maquoketa Caves State Park

The witness, Mark, told Linda Godfrey that he'd had a previous experience with something odd during a spelunking trip in Mexico in 2002. That experience, detailed in Godfrey's book *I Know What I Saw*, was an odd one but didn't prepare the man for the encounter in his home state.

Maquoketa Caves State Park is a popular spot for outdoors enthusiasts and is the most visited park in the state. It covers about 370 acres and has thirteen caves for people to explore. The park is south of Dubuque in Jackson County.

Mark was exploring one of the caves that summer day and had his young daughter with him. It was a Tuesday, so there were few tourists and Mark reports that they mostly had the park to themselves. He recalls:

"It happened pretty fast...I was about fifty yards away from my daughter inside the lower Dance Hall cave, just exploring and climbing around. I was taking pictures of the cave, and something just popped up between my daughter and me. It was tall and skinny with a really long neck and long arms too. It was completely naked."

Mark told Godfrey that he snapped a picture, and the thing

209

quickly took off. Believing that his daughter could be in danger, Mark moved as fast as he could over to her. The girl had not seen the creature.

The entire incident was puzzling on many levels. The fact that the park has so many visitors leads one to wonder why more people have not reported any strange creatures. Then again, perhaps the things are very adept at staying concealed. Mark notes that he has explored the caves extensively over the years and had never seen such a thing previously.

He says the incident has never left his mind, and he speculates that the things may live deep underground in places that humans just aren't accessing. He says that he believes in subterranean creatures but has a hard time understanding their existence in Iowa. Still, there are plenty of possibilities. Mark states:

"Perhaps this creature can squeeze like a mouse can under a doorway. I have many theories about Iowa's caves, that they are all somehow connected to a larger system. One system has been explored for forty years and no end is in sight."

Mark's photo shows a strange figure. It appears to be a small, thin-necked, bald humanoid standing in the cave. Doubters will say the figure is that of another person, but Mark didn't try to gain publicity from the sighting and he remains puzzled by the encounter.

Weird Humanoids

MONSTERS OF THE HAWKEYE STATE by David Weatherly

Acknowledgements

A very special thanks to my friends Chad Lewis and Kevin Lee Nelson for their invaluable assistance on this volume of the Monsters of America series. Both these gentlemen are outstanding researchers and share my passion for pursuing the weird.

An additional thanks goes out to Kevin Lee Nelson for the great foreword he provided for this book.

As always, I continue to be grateful for the support and input of my friends and colleagues as this series continues to progress, including Loren Coleman, Dr. Jeff Meldrum, John LeMay, Lyle Blackburn, Ken Gerhard, Nick Redfern, Paul Bestall, Albert Rosales and Jay Bachochin.

Thanks to Mister Sam Shearon for yet another fantastic cover for the series, Eddie at SMAK Graphics for layout and Jerry Hajewski for editing.

Last but certainly not least, thanks to the many witnesses and organizations who have shared their sightings, opinions, and information.

Bibliography

Crowe, Ray. Bigfoot Behavior Volume II. CreateSpace Independent Publishing, Scotts Valley, CA. 2015.

Flaherty, Ray. Our Lizard Creek Farm. Vantage Press, Burlington, VT. 1969.

Godfrey, Linda. I Know What I Saw: Modern-Day Encounters with Monsters of New Urban Legend and Ancient Lore. TarcherPerigee, New York, NY. 2020.

Green, John. Sasquatch: the Apes Among Us. Hancock House Publishers, Surrey, British Columbia 2006.

Hicks, Bernice, and Woodbury, Ruby. Douglas Township Historical Story. Douglas Township Historical Society.

Laundre, John W. Phantoms of the Prairie: The Return of Cougars to the Midwest. University of Wisconsin Press, Madison, WI. 2012.

Lewis, Chad and Fisk, Terry. The Iowa Road Guide to Haunted Locations. Unexplained Research, Eau Claire, WI. 2007.

Lewis, Chad, Voss, Noah, and Nelson, Kevin Lee. The Van Meter Visitor: A True and Mysterious Encounter with the Unknown. On the Road Publications, Eau Claire, WI. 2013.

Newton, Michael. Encyclopedia of Cryptozoology. McFarland & Company, Jefferson, NC. 2005.

Pielak, Lori. Ghosts of Dallas County. Quixote Press, Weaver, Ia. 2003.

Rife, Philip. Bigfoot Across America. Writers Club Press, Lincoln, NE 2000.

Steiger, Brad, and Steiger, Sherry Hansen. Haunted: Malevolent Ghosts, Night Terrors, and Threatening Phantoms. Visible Ink

Press, Canton Charter Township, MI. 2018.

Steiger, Brad. Real Monsters, Gruesome Critters, and Beasts from the Darkside. Visible Ink Press, Canton Charter Township, MI. 2010.

Steiger, Brad, and Steiger, Sherry Hansen. Starborn. Berkley Books, New York, NY. 1992.

Publications

Iowa Historian Newsletter Spring 2003

Pursuit #62

Sasquatch Report March 1997

UFO Report Summer 1975

Websites

Cryptozoonews

National UFO Reporting Center

Sasquatch Chronicles

Bibliography

Photo Credits

Rock Island Depot, Van Meter image courtesy of Grinnell College Historic Iowa Postcard Collection, special collections and archives. File:Rock Island Depot, Van Meter, Iowa.jpg - Wikimedia Commons

Wapsipinicon River at Independence, Buchanan County photo by James C. Orvis, B & W conversion, via Wikimedia commons File:Wapsipinicon River viewed from the Okoboji Grill, Independence, Buchanan County, Iowa Sunday, August 25, 2013 1.JPG - Wikimedia Commons

Special thanks to Kevin Lee Nelson for his drawing of the Van Meter Visitor.

All other photos copyright author or are held in the public domain.

About the Author

David Weatherly is a renaissance man of the strange and supernatural. He has traveled the world in pursuit of ghosts, cryptids, UFOs, magic, and more. From the specters of dusty castles, to remote, haunted islands, from ancient sites to modern mysteries, he has journeyed to the most unusual places on the globe seeking the unknown.

David became fascinated with the paranormal at a young age. Ghost stories and accounts of weird creatures and UFOs led him to discover many of his early influences. Writers such as John Keel, Jacques Vallee, Hans Holzer, and others set him on course to spend his life exploring and investigating the unexplained.

Throughout his life, he's also delved into shamanic and magical traditions from around the world, spending time with elders from numerous cultures in Europe, the Americas, Africa, and Asia. He has studied with Taoist masters in China, Tibetan Lamas, and other mystics from the far east. He's picked up knowledge from African and Native American tribal elders and sat around fires with shamans from countless other traditions.

Along his path, David has also gathered a lot of arcane knowledge, studying a range of ancient arts from palmistry, the runes, and other obscure forms of divination, to alchemy and magick. He has studied and taught Qigong and Ninjutsu, as well as various energy related arts. David has also studied stage and performance magic.

His shamanic and magical background has given him a unique perspective in his explorations into the unknown, and he continues to write, travel, and explore, leaving no stone unturned in his quest for the strange and unusual.

David has investigated, and written about, a diverse range of topics, including, Hauntings & Ghosts, Cryptozoology, Ufology, Ancient Mysteries, Shamanism, Magic, and Psychic Phenomena.

David is the founder of the independent media and publishing company, Eerie Lights Publishing.

He has been a featured speaker at conferences around the world and has lectured for countless paranormal and spiritual groups.

He is a frequent guest on *Coast to Coast AM* with George Noory, *Spaced Out Radio* and other radio programs. David has also appeared on numerous television shows including the Travel Channel's *Mysteries of the Outdoors*, History Channel's *Ancient Aliens*, *Beyond Belief* and other programs. He was also featured in the highly successful series *On the Trail of UFOs*.

David's books include *Strange Intruders, Eerie Companions,* the *Monsters of America* series, and the *Haunted* series.

Find David online at:

https://eerielights.com

Made in the USA
Monee, IL
10 March 2024

54803464R00136